In *No Longer Dis-Eve'd,* Angela Berton cardiologist," dives deeper into the emotion intended to use our eternal spiritual life force to heal and to live the lives of passion, intimacy, and abundant joy He desires for us. With stark honesty, Bertone shares the painful and prayerful quest she and her husband, Michael, courageously embarked on in an effort to heal their broken hearts so that they could experience the true gift of marriage and secure the scriptural promise of life abundant. The author gives a brilliant and concise analysis and explanation of the important function of our emotions while skillfully incorporating biblical study and scholarship to create a transcendent prescription for intimacy in all of our relationships.

As a follow-up to her bold and lively first book, *Good Mourning Sunshine,* a wakeup call and primer for personal transformation, *No Longer Dis-Eve'd* explores more deeply how we can access the treasures stored within our emotions and the spiritual promise that is fulfilled through understanding them. This beautifully crafted short masterpiece is right on the mark. Full of "aha" moments and revelation for the reader, *No Longer Dis-Eve'd* will most certainly start a revolution in understanding how God truly uses a part of us that is eternal—our emotions—to heal and transform our relationship with Him and all of our relationships.

Ming Lovejoy
Health Coach and Educator

The creation of man is recorded in Genesis 2:1-9. In verse 7 it is stated, "And the Lord God formed man of the dust of the ground, and breathed into his nostrils the breath of life; and man became a living soul." From this act of creation, we are made up of body, soul, and spirit. We are well acquainted with our body. However, our soulish and spirit natures are foreign to us. Yet out of these flow all the issues of life.In this book, Angela, like a skilled surgeon, separates the soul and the spirit and shows through example how these control our lives. Various viruses attack our soul through life and lead us in a self-destructive life style. Unless these viruses are attacked through the spirit life and God's Spirit, we limp through life wounded and unfulfilled. This book is a must read for those in search of a full and complete life!

Robert D. Ross
Former pastor and traveling minister, member of Board of Presbyters for the Assemblies of God, and board of Regents for North Central University, Minneapolis, Minnesota, and Northwest University, Seattle, Washington

"My friend and sister in Christ allows you into her heart and soul from the deepest fear to the unbelievable joy. This is a must-read. If you get through the first chapter and don't see the love she has for God and the growing of the unconditional love for Michael, you might need a pacemaker. This line from the book is permanently etched in my mind and soul: "This belief system is creating my current reality, which is filled with abundance and joy while living on the edge of my seat." Bless yourself with reading a raw look into the life of a Christian woman who finally heard God speak."

Yvette Richards
Former National President of UMW 2012-2016

Angela Bertone illustrates not one but two extraordinary areas of expertise and masterfully blends the worlds of Christianity with human behavior in an unparalleled way. Her vulnerability, authenticity, and critical thinking offers a work that is insightful and thought provoking. Topics not often covered are shared with an openness and bravery that simply has to be applauded.

Lynda Cormier-Hanser
Speaker, Author, Co-CEO, Gia Wellness

What a great resource *No Longer Dis-Eved* is for any marriage walking the journey to true intimacy! As a Christian psychotherapist, a marriage counselor, and a minister of inner healing and deliverance for over twenty-five years, I appreciate not only the truth-based wisdom found in these pages but Angela's open vulnerability, and humility, with which she shares it. *No Longer Dis-Eved* takes a refreshingly Christ-focused approach to the difficult and often neglected subjects of Christian sexuality and marital intimacy with practicality and depth at the same time. Angela cuts past the annoying and religious quick fixes found in many other Christian marriage books of the day and exposes the codependency and idolatry of marriage in our Christian culture that is at the root of many of our false expectations that lead to relational division. Be prepared to be challenged in your marriage and sexuality in a very practical sense, but even more so to be called higher and deeper in your intimacy with Christ Jesus as His bride.

Steve Fair, LMSW
Director of Renewal Christian Counseling Center, Author, *The Journey into the Divided Heart*

No Longer
DIS-Eve'd

Finding the Pathway
to Emotional Intimacy

ANGELA BERTONE

3FOLDMEDiA

ISBN: 978-1-942056-63-8

Library of Congress Control Number: 2018932256

Printed in the USA

I dedicate this book to my husband, Michael Bertone Sr., who loved me when I did not feel loveable. As we prepared our wedding vows, we both loved the Scripture where Adam called Eve "bone of my bones." Today, we both agree this remains the verse that sums up our union.

Two broken and bruised hearts came together in the union of holy matrimony and now testify together in our story that when we suffer *together*, in Jesus, we shall also reign *together with Him*.

Thank you, Michael, for your blessing and support; I needed to write our story with transparency and vulnerability. You have trusted me with your heart and I have prayerfully endeavored to honor it with humility and the graces of our God.

Moreover, I want to thank all the men and women who have taught us so much about the marriage union by trusting us to be your spiritual coaches over the years. Your sorrows and sufferings have helped us to see our own issues with a deeper clarity and understanding. We are honored to have shared in your stories.

Acknowledgments

I would like to thank everyone who labored with me through the birthing of this book; to all who read my unedited chapters and gave honest feedback as well as much-needed encouragement. Those who provoked my studies, commented in my classes, pushed me to expand my verbiage, and who kept asking me, "When will it be finished?"

Moreover, I want to express my gratitude to Marlaine Peachey, CMA, who worked after hours to insure I would have my manuscript edited and ready by deadline. Your critique was greatly needed and much appreciated. Thank you for keeping my head above the waters.

Thank you to my pastors, Chuck and Sha DeGruy at The Gathering Place International in Albany, Louisiana, for supporting me in ministry and lovingly directing my path along this journey. Thank you for introducing me to Brian and Candice Simmons, who introduced me to 5 Fold Media.

Thank you, Brian and Candice, for allowing me to share my story over lunch and encouraging me to write these things to share with others. Thank you for introducing me to Andy and Cathy Sanders, who are as wonderful as you promised they would be.

To Andy, Cathy, and the 5 Fold Media team, thank you for all that you have done and are doing to help authors like me to produce professional works to inspire the world.

Contents

Foreword

No Longer Dis-Eve'd is a book that looks at our emotions and how our emotions are the window into our relationships with ourselves, our spouses, others, and God. So often we have been taught that our emotions are not to be trusted and in fact are the source of many of our problems; however, Angela takes a fresh look at how our emotions can be the source of transformation as we come to experience the true source of our value. Angela illuminates that we have two minds that are often at odds with each other. First there is the logical mind that strives to calculate and control our thoughts and emotions and often leaves us broken and stuck in past patterns and beliefs. Then there is the heart mind, which is the source of our beliefs and is foundational in transforming our lives. Often these beliefs and emotions are based on past experiences and the perceptions we attached to the events of our earlier life. Unless our emotional memory is given new information, then we are doomed to be triggered by events that resemble our past. It is only when we experience God's unconditional love in our emotions that we become free.

No Longer Dis-Eve'd takes a look at our judgments, which we are bound to manifest in our own lives. Our judgments and self-awareness become the portal into humility and forgiveness manifested in gratitude. In addition, our sorrows and sufferings are no longer emotions to avoid but rather opportunities for us to connect with Jesus in His sufferings. This allows our sufferings to become the doorway toward intimacy with God and to experience His understanding and love.

In No Longer Dis-Eve'd, we are invited on a journey of healing and intimacy with ourselves, our spouses, others, and most importantly

God. Transformation becomes obtainable and freedom becomes possible. Thank you, Angela, for this journey into emotional healing.

Daniel E. Munzing, M.D.,
Associate Clinical Professor, University of Washington School of Medicine

Introduction

When we study the Bible from the English translations, though we hold it to be the true Word of God, we are not able to dig as deep into the meanings of the Scriptures as when studied from the Hebrew. The Hebrew language has pictures, numbers, history, math, and homonyms; additionally, each letter is like a scroll in and of itself.

As you read this work, I want you to know that I wrote it from the perspective that I derived by studying all the above. You may experience an expression of the Scriptures unlike any you have seen before. I encourage you to explore the Hebrew language and see for yourself if what I am sharing holds to the truth of the infallible Word of God.

The Bible tells us that treasures are hidden by God in darkness, but kings will search them out. Were you aware that the entire creation is revealing the unseen mysteries of God, including the eternal Godhead and His power? It says that it is clearly seen and that we are without excuse.

Have you seen the eternal Godhead and power? It is right before our eyes, revealed in the second letter of the Hebrew alphabet. *Bet* is the first letter used in the Torah, and it means "two" and "house or dwelling place." This is not the only meaning of the letter *bet*, but to keep with the integrity of this work I will not discuss all the meanings here.

God made man as His dwelling place. Our human bodies are called temples as well as tents. Moreover, we are told in the Bible that we are in Him and He is in us. The pattern of the two in one can be seen in all of creation. We will be focused primarily on Christ in us to understand the mystery of humans as the bride of Christ.

God created Adam, who was two, with Eve hidden inside of Adam. They were the two, even though Eve was not yet manifested. The Bible says that Adam was made in God's likeness and image, both male and female, two in one. Their very nature declares duality, yet we also know that Jesus was

13

present as He always was, is, and is yet to come. Even though duality alone cannot reveal all of God, we will be looking at duality to understand a part of God that is revealed in the creation of Adam.

In keeping with the theme of the word "two" revealing part of the nature of mankind, let's take note of the second letter of the Hebrew alphabet: *Bet*. It is fitting that not only is its place value two, but its numerical value is also two. Some terms used to define *Bet* are "dwelling place, house, household, tent, building, and tabernacle." Ancient Hebrew developed as a pictorial language, wherein the letters and words represented pictures in addition to sounds. The letter *Bet* has a form that is the shape of the tent of meetings used by Moses in the wilderness. This is where he met with God.

In the marital relationship between man and woman, the two become one in the body which is, in fact, a tent or dwelling place for the soul. God also promises to dwell in our bodies as His dwelling place. God promised David that God Himself would make an eternal household for the throne of David. He was speaking of Jesus as the first temple where God would dwell forever and how He would later dwell in us through our union with Jesus. It is fitting that the first book of both the Torah and the Bible begins with the account of God creating the heavens and the earth—two dwelling places.

Another president that supports the hidden mysteries of the "two" is the Jewish teaching concerning the phrase "in the beginning" found in the Torah. Genesis 1:1 in the King James Version reads: "In the beginning." The first book—and the first word—in the Torah is *b'reshith*, which means, "in a beginning." Therefore, the Hebrew word *b'ereshit* means "in the beginning," and as the head of all things (the house, the dwelling place), God created the heaven (the lofty {to be high, higher}, the aloft, the air, the astrologer) and the Earth (the field, the ground, the nations, the wilderness, the world). Notice these are all dwelling places, just like the letter *Bet* indicates. Together, the first and second letters of the alphabet reveal the head of the house and the house itself united as one.

Note that Jesus taught us to pray for the unity of heaven and Earth in the Lord's prayer. I am amazed at the layers of how God used word to create. We express words in something that we call the alphabet: the *Aleph*, meaning the head of the house and the beginning, and *Bet*, meaning in the dwelling where the two abide. Duality is expressed in the letter *Bet*, for what good is a dwelling without someone to dwell in it? Moreover, the letter *Aleph* has within its meaning the word aloof. It means to be just out of our understanding—as God is unseen and *aloof*, yet still dwelling in the house. Herein lies the understanding that God is both seen and unseen; in heaven everyone can see God, but on earth God must be revealed. Maybe one of the reasons the letter Bet is used prior to the letter *Aleph* in the Torah is that without an opposite, we could neither see nor comprehend the difference between the one who dwells in us and ourselves as the dwelling place in which God resides.

Aleph also means "leader, Father" and is known as the beginning. *Aleph* explains how God will manifest His power through the man in humility. It also holds within its meaning the number one, which means unity. Note: in order to experience unity, more than one would be needed to show the nature of unity. In addition, disunity would also need to exist in order to understand the nature of unity.

This could explain why Adam was both male and female, yet was combined in one body until God separated them into two human beings. As declared in the mystery of the marriage, "the two shall become one flesh." So, we could conclude that God is two in one who, when fully manifested, was seen in the Son, namely Jesus. Without the two we could not have the Son, and without the Son we could not see the love and unity of God. Therefore, just like the rabbis teach, without duality it would be impossible to see God's loving nature.

"I form the light, and create darkness; I make peace, and create evil. I am Jehovah, that doeth all these things" (Isaiah 45:7 ASV). The creation of darkness also shows God's goodness. With only light in our eyes, we would not be able to see, as our pupils would contract to squeeze out the light, and if that did not work we would shield our eyes instinctively to avoid the pain of excess light. Would you place your newborn child out in the sunlight without the protection of the shade? Of course not. If we who are evil, according to the Bible, would shield our children from excess light, how much more would our heavenly Father cover us with mercy by creating darkness.

Jesus spoke in parables. He only spoke what He heard the Father say, so we can conclude that Father spoke in parables. Because of this truth, we can be confident that heavenly mysteries are hidden in the creation, as well as in the true earthly stories of the Bible. We are instructed to not look at what we can see but to look intently at what we cannot see. "And I know that his commandment is life everlasting: whatsoever I speak therefore, even as the Father said unto me, so I speak" (John 12:50 KJV). "Then said Jesus unto them, When ye have lifted up the Son of man, then shall ye know that I am he, and that I do nothing of myself; but as my Father hath taught me, I speak these things" (John 8:28 KJV). "While we look not at the things which are seen, but at the things which are not seen: for the things which are seen are temporal; but the things which are not seen are eternal" (2 Corinthians 4:18 KJV).

This introduction was to open the pathway for looking at the unseen things. We will do this through that which is seen, using parables both in stories and in God's creation. Let's look for the mysteries that have been hidden by God in the marriage union.

Chapter 1: Keeping Up Appearances

What I am about to share will be very candid, yet respecting what God has called holy. Michael, my husband, and I have agreed to share our stories about our marriage. In addition to discussing emotional intimacy, this book will cover the topic of sexual intimacy. I write this with tremendous honor not only for my marriage, but honor for the marriage union as God has established it. Often this topic is shied away from in an effort to not offend. It is my endeavor to write and speak on this topic in a way that will bring about healing to marriages and revelation of the male and the female image of God. The woman is to be a helpmate in many ways and she is to reveal the glory of man while man is revealing the glory of God. It is my intention to unveil this intimacy in such a manner that the deep mysteries of heartfelt intimacy can be experienced in wholeness with God and man, with mankind being the bride of Christ.

Sexual intimacy in the union of a man and a woman is designed to be an outward, physical, mirror-image expression of our inward emotional intimacy. In fact, sexual intimacy without emotional intimacy will not satisfy the human soul. I had never been taught this. In fact, I was trained to avoid my emotions because they were fleshly and could lead me astray. It wasn't until my marriage began to fall apart that I took the risk and followed my heart. It was only then that my marriage began to experience healing and eventually wholeness.

Before the fall, intimacy was without judgment and shame. Humans were spiritually alive and spiritually intimate with God and each other. In our separation from God and in our shame and guilt, people often have sex without experiencing emotional oneness.

Have you ever had sex in order to feel loved or accepted? Did it work? Did the feelings last? Maybe you have had sex to protect your spouse from feeling rejected. Would you want someone to have sex with you out of pity? Moreover, how satisfying is it to be responsible for another person's self-worth? Has sex been a duty or commitment to your marriage vows? If you answered yes to any of these, you are not alone. This doesn't sound like life abundant, nor peace and joy. This sounds like slavery to me. Does this portray the relationship that Jesus has with His bride? Absolutely not.

It was our knowledge of good and evil that robbed us of our emotional union, which is spiritual. Instead we became intellectual, relying on our judgments to guide us and keep peace in our relationships.

I humbly invite you into our hearts as we share our story with you. Though much of this work will focus on our pain, please rest assured it was suffering together that has paved the way for the current joys of our relationship with God and each other. Michael and I had both built walls of protection around our emotions. Why not? Who wants to feel rejection and failure? With our hearts hidden behind these walls, it didn't take long before we both felt the separation of our self-protecting.

Our hearts were aware of this separation and were always crying out for attention. We are no different from anyone else, so we stayed busy, trying to quiet our emotions. We both sought comfort in each other's arms and often felt safe in our marriage. Early on we took up the opinion that we were both suffering from dysfunctional family issues, but we had agreed to face them and never give up. We both adored each other and quite often stumbled into our original passions for each other. In fact, it was our passion that kept us fighting to stay in love. He loved me when I didn't love myself and that was worth fighting to keep.

As our life together began, I took the role of the good wife, and he stepped into the function of the hard-working provider. We shared the same morals, basic religious beliefs, work ethics, and love for the traditional family. We took our vows to heart and planned on taking them to the grave. I often asked God, "Are you sure I can't stay married to him in heaven?" To my delight, Michael agreed with that prayer.

Even though we had all of this going for us, we quickly became aware of the crazy baggage we had carried into our holy union. In our tenacity and awareness of our issues, we turned to God early in our marriage, asking Him to help us. Our physical eyes and ears were not able to see or hear God, but we were determined to have faith.

We had never been taught that God had equipped us with emotional eyes and ears or that they were trapped in a calloused heart of stone. In this condition, we vacillated between our intellect, sexuality, and our emotions in our efforts to keep our passion alive. Society, movies, songs, and even religion had taught us what made a house a home, and that included the notion that healthy sexual pleasure will produce intimacy. Women were even taught that this was a means to make their husbands happy and that it was their wifely duty. The problem is, our religion, leaders, society, traditions, and famous people who were, by default, mentoring and/or teaching us how to have a successful marriage didn't show any signs of a successful marriage. Our contentment wavered over the years, and only in heightened states of emotional pain did true changes take us over our obstacles, where we would come up for air grateful to still be passionately in love. I must admit, there were times when neither of us were sure if our marriage would survive.

We both agree now that marriage is a physical and emotional union that can open the eyes of our heart. This is the only relational union that God used in Scripture as an expression of Jesus and His bride. Jesus is spirit and has a spiritual/emotional union with us. We, as humans, are physical and spiritual. Therefore, we are able to experience both. Only after we tasted both spiritual and emotional connection within our physical union were we able to understand each of them. It was kind of like we had to taste the bitter pain of the physical breakdown in our marriage in order to seek, discover, and then appreciate the sweetness of a spiritual/emotional union. Neither of us had ever considered that our spiritual union was the real and that our physical union was a mirror image. Spontaneous, passionate, buckle-my-knees kind of love—now that is sweet. Who wants duty after that? This process makes me think of chocolate and the beauty of bitter and sweet united. No wonder it is a symbol of love, for true love endures the bitterness and trusts in all things.

Sexual union is one of the most powerful relationships known to man. It can bring about deep intimate satisfaction, but it can also be a source of sorrow, suffering, and disappointment. The only other expression of intimacy that holds such extreme power is the bond between a parent and a child. This is not surprising, as the child is the manifestation of the physical union of the married couple. No wonder God created the sexual union and childbearing in the very beginning. Was God showing us, in Genesis, a picture of the marriage without emotion? Was their desire to trust knowledge the beginning of their sorrows?

I didn't realize that the story of Adam and Eve would ever affect me so deeply. How could Adam's sorrow and the sweat of his brow, coupled with his hunger, play a part in my marriage? Moreover, how could Eve's multiplied sorrows in the bringing forth of children relate other than in childbirth? Could they have a deeper spiritual meaning?

I can see how both results were manifested in the planting and reaping of seed. I also understand that God made them from the soil. Is it possible that the soil of my flesh was cursed, and those curses could pass down to my children though the seed?

Note that Jesus referred to talking to God as eating, and He called Himself manna from heaven. Adam and Eve gave up the heavenly manna from God and turned to knowledge. If we eat from our knowledge, will it cause us to work to please God and, by the sweat of our brow, remain under the curse of the knowledge tree? Never attaining, praying and praying, hoping one day God will hear us for our many words.

We are called His bride. Could bearing children in sorrow also have a spiritual meaning? As we continue, keep in mind that God's word is seed and our hearts are the place where God would put His seed of truth. Early in our marriage we began to hide the Word of God in our hearts and did our best to do good and avoid evil. I had convinced myself that because I was attempting to obey God, my marriage would be good. I was not yet aware that, like Eve, my desire was for my husband over God, and I was using Michael's love toward me to feel whole. I was establishing my identity in being Michael's wife. I justified it by making sure that I would be a godly one for sure. I had bought into the illusion that love was an action and a commitment that Michael and I could give to each other, and that would please God. My pride and self-righteousness was pretty sneaky. Marriage was a beautiful setup to return me to God. It was only after I sought with all of my heart to find wholeness through Michael that I discovered I could never find it there. In his failure to be my god, my heart had grown weary and disillusioned. Because of the fact that we were focused on our outward measurements of success—well behaved children, nice home, two cars, a healthy bank account, as well as social and religious status—I had no idea my heart was waxing cold on the inside.

One afternoon, I was making an avocado sandwich on a corn tortilla for myself. Being the good wife that I was, I offered some to my husband.

"No," he said, "but I would really like it if you put some in that really good homemade salad dressing that you make."

"OK. Let me know if you change your mind."

I returned to the kitchen and made my sandwich, never thinking twice about his request for avocado salad.

This may not seem like a big deal, but in times past that would never have happened. You see, while he was still being my god, I would have sacrificed my sandwich and made his salad in a heartbeat. But not on that day. Moreover, I was numb to my response.

Later that night while I was making supper, I remembered his request for avocado salad. Feeling like the good wife again, I cut up the avocado and began taking all of the ingredients out of the cupboard to make "that really good homemade salad dressing" that he liked. However, before I could blink an eye, I thought, "I have some store bought dressing in the fridge; I don't need to waste my time." I put all of the fresh ingredients back in the cupboard. Then, to my surprise, I heard God speak in my heart.

"Angela, why did you do that?"

"I don't know God; why did I?"

"Because you are going in and out of a coma and your love will soon die if you don't attend to it."

"Oh no! God, please help me!"

"I am, right now. I am giving you eyes to see. You are blind, and without Me you cannot see."

I was eating from learned experiences of the knowledge of good and evil. I had become tired and weary of Michael not fulfilling my expectations of a god. In fact, I had actually transitioned into trying to be his Holy Spirit. I made it my job to let him know just how much of a failure he had become. Let me tell you how I justified my behavior: I was a good wife. (You remember, the godly kind.) Actually, I was proud and arrogant, and my attitude was terrible, even though I was doing all the right things. This was to make sure that Michael could not blame me. Maybe he would see how wonderful I was and start to appreciate me.

Denial still amazes me today. When I was attempting to manipulate Michael into being my god, I told myself that it was my duty to serve him. I even used the Bible to justify my unhealthy behavior. In fact, most of the women in my life lived the same way. I knew they were not happy, but I could not figure out why. I was under the illusion that they were doing the godly thing. This was common in our culture, and anyone who questioned it was frowned upon.

To be honest, I kept expecting it to work for me and was frustrated when it didn't yield the results I desired. In fact, I had no idea that I was keeping score and was attempting to trade him for love and acceptance. I was not aware that this behavior was codependent nor destructive. Moreover, it was not until the avocado salad incident that I had any inkling that I had moved out of codependency and into self-sufficiency. I had gone from being a codependent, groveling worm to an independent "B," and I don't mean babe. The hypocrisy of my delusions disgusts me as I look back. I had become like the serpent worm that deceived Eve. Eating my own dust, as I like to call it, or eating from the tree of the knowledge of good and evil could never bring about a fulfilling relationship. Just as God had warned Adam, knowledge without God could never nourish us. In fact, eating dust had caused me to hunger and thirst and seek for deeper fulfilling relationship. The really sad part is that I actually believed that I was doing all the right things. I was totally blind to my self-righteousness. Only here could I begin to understand how God could take what was meant for evil against me and use it for my good. My distaste for dust birthed a desire to return to God and intimacy.

I am so glad that God has promised to use all things for our good, and eventually we shall see He was in all things from the beginning. What glory! I didn't understand this, though I surely quoted it. In Genesis, it states that the curse would last for "all" of the days of "his (Adam's) life." The word "all" here means until he is **complete or made perfect**. God was not punishing them. On the contrary, He was ensuring that they would return or be perfected in sorrow. This is why Jesus said if you suffer with Me, you shall reign with Me. The words "his life" are talking about the fact that they were living from their own dust—knowledge, intellect, and reasoning. I was most definitely eating from my own dust. My marriage was becoming dry and I was starting to use my children, my work, and "my ministry" to escape the pain of my marriage. It breaks my heart that I was actually teaching others the art of being good and avoiding even the appearance of evil, and then you will be blessed with a good life and that included a good marriage. My heart truly loved God, my husband, and others, and the intent of my heart was pure. My methods, however, didn't work for me. I now realize they never worked from the beginning with Adam and Eve either.

The problem is that I was teaching through religion, not love. You know, looking back, my friends admit now that I made them feel like they could never measure up. They knew I loved them but rarely felt it.

The truth in my eyes was becoming as painful as sand. It was time to lay down my own understanding. I no longer had an appetite to eat from my dry dust nature. I became hungry for truth and emotional intimacy. It was time to return to the land of the living, where bloody, emotional, heartfelt relationship is. This kind of relationship is only found in Christ, and this life was now calling me.

How can suffering be the pathway to our return to God? Hadn't I suffered enough? Now I was in a coma and I had already done all that I knew to do. It was time to let go in order to "**receive**" from God. After all, isn't that what God created Adam and Eve to be? Weren't we all created as human *receivers* of God's love? It was costing me everything, my marriage being the first thing that God was asking me to let go of. He had been asking for years, but I was afraid.

Every part of life requires us to let go in order to mature and experience fullness of joy. Everything that multiplies must first divide. Now God was asking me to die in order to live. That is why Jesus said unless a grain of wheat falls into the ground and dies, it will not produce fruit, and if we desire to live, we must die.

Life in this earth presents us with mirrors of our soul to help us awaken to our condition. A man can only see himself by looking at his reflection. These mirrors had come to me from the laws of sowing and reaping, judging and becoming, believing and having, thinking and being, and holding on to eventually let go. They are all messengers designed to point me back to God.

No Longer Dis-Eve'd

These messengers of truth are usually painful and often brutal. In fact, I had run from them at times only to return to the same mirror, my reflection now magnified and filled with sorrow.

God was not punishing me; rather, His mercies were pointing me back to the truth. God was about to awaken my realization of His love for me. Moreover, He was restoring my identity in Him. The truth plus nothing was about to set me free. The truth that Michael and I were about to face was going to kill us so that we could arise and have the passion in our marriage that reflected Christ and His bride.

Notice the word. *Opposite*. It means light and darkness in order to see. When God created Eve, he created Adam's opposite. In the Hebrew, it actually says **his oppose**. Well, Michael and I were about to see just how painful that could be.

Through the sorrows of marriage, we are compelled to face our issues or end the union. Unfortunately, most jump ship because they are not aware that the very sorrow they are running from is needed in order to heal. Seeing the truth of our own soul is our only hope for life abundant. The Kingdom of God is where we were headed, and God was about to invite us to abide there.

On a side note, this part inside us, in our heart, is like the womb. It bleeds to clean and prepare for the seed. Our hearts were most definitely about to bleed. God's word/seed was about to go into the darkness of my heart and Michael's to reveal truth. This was a good thing, but what we would see would devastate us at first.

Early one morning I was making my bed. My children were at school and Michael was working. I had my music up loud and I was enjoying my time with God alone. As I ran my hands across the crisp white sheets, I heard God say, "If you are able, I will show you deep mysteries upon this canvas." I froze for a moment and pondered the question. This was around 1997, and the last time God offered me such mysteries was 10 years prior. Back then, I was creeped out and actually thought it was wicked and refused to believe God would speak to me about sex. At the age of twenty-one, talking to God about sex was sort of like talking to my dad about sex. I was not interested. I would much rather talk to my mom. At that time in my life, I couldn't even consider God bringing up the subject at all, much less being "married" to Jesus.

Angela Bertone

It was only after I had the experience of a parent who told her own child about "the birds and the bees" that I was able to listen to God. I was reminded of how after I broke the news to my son, explaining where he came from and how he got in my tummy, he responded, "Are you and Daddy going to have any more babies?"

"No," I replied.

"Well good! Then you never have to do that again." That must have seemed really creepy to his little heart. I broke into laughter, understanding his innocence prevented him from seeing the beauty of such union. God had waited ten years for me, and I am convinced He would have waited longer if I needed Him to.

With that in mind, and still with some apprehension, I agreed to God's request and was willing to learn about the deeper hidden truths of the sexual union. For the first time, I was truly open to understanding the mysteries of marriage spoken of in the book of Ephesians.

Sometimes the revelation was simple and painless, but often it was through the sorrows of my marriage that God would teach me about being the bride of Christ. I could not see how I could be reaping such sorrows. After all, weren't the promises of God and the positive confessions of my mouth, declaring the Word of God over my life, supposed to protect me?

I didn't know that my heart had a brain and that I was double-minded. I had no idea that my feelings were more powerful than my logic and that I was creating the mirrors in my life. I looked for someone or something to blame, because I was "doing" all the right things, the way I had been taught. I could no longer blame my husband, so I would often blame the devil. Neither of these responses yielded lasting change. No wonder my misery continued. The truth was waking me up; however, my primitive desire to fight or run would get the best of me, and like Adam and Eve I just wanted to run and hide from the truth. Remember, Jesus called Himself "the Truth."

Years earlier, God had begun to show me that my relationship with Michael was a mirror image of my relationship with my husband Jesus. In my ignorance and pride, I argued with God and proceeded to tell Him how great our relationship was. I concluded that Michael was the reason I was having such difficulties. I argued, "If Michael would treat me like Christ treated the Church, then we would not be having all these problems." In time, it became very clear to me that God is not mocked, and I was only reaping in my earthy marriage what I was sowing in my spiritual relationship to Christ. This was devastating, as you will soon see. Truth soon held me captive and humility became my robes. For example, I would spend most of my prayer time complaining to God about Michael, angry that all Michael did was complain. Really? How blind could I be?

You may say, "No way! I would never treat God like my husband treats me. God and I have a great relationship! That may have been true for you, but not me." I understand. If God had not revealed it to me, I would have never believed it either. Many of my friends now confess that it was true for them too. They would be disgusted at their own self-deceptions as shame and humility began to heal them of the same lies. This kind of revelation I call "The Brutal Truth."

In years past, when I used marriage and sexuality as an allegory for our relationship with Jesus, I attracted much criticism and many objections. Even today, I still have naysayers who object to my position in the matter. Some of you who read this work may feel uncomfortable and even offended. I understand, and I suggest that if the thought of this is repulsive, in time you may change your mind and realize that unless this part of us is made whole, our relationships will suffer. In fact, you may be very happy in your relationships. If so, I rejoice with you. However, for the sake of the many who are struggling and wounded, I take the risk and open my heart to you in this work.

The abundance of sexual perversions in our society and the fears of being misunderstood that hindered me discussing this topic candidly in times past are no longer a hurdle for me. The temptations to remain silent and avoid the backlash are weaker than the passions in me to set people free. I have suffered much rejection and rebuke, which have only caused me to dig deeper and study harder. I now consider it an honor to present this truth that has liberated my soul. I refuse to allow fear to keep couples bound by unhealthy relationships and calloused hearts, without remedy when they want the same freedom I have experienced.

We have entered into the time of the unveiling of the bride. Put on your brave hearts and settle no longer. Survival is not our portion. Life abundant is. Let us take courage and endure the pains of life until the true God-nature in us is birthed, revealing the sons of God, who are His bride.

The act of sex is not lovemaking. We must return to God's design and avoid using sex as a means to an end. By using sex, it has become a drug, commitment, method, business, duty, and a means of control and manipulation. Escaping the truth is not possible, and using sex as a means of control will eventually end in destruction of us as individuals and as a society.

For many couples, the thought of a holy, joyful, passionate, abundant marriage remains only a dream—a treasure hoped for but seldom attained. Many of our children don't even want to get married. This is because so many have suffered the sorrows of a failed one. Yet only when opposites come together as ordained by God is dunamis (power) seen, experienced, realized, and understood. When Jesus was questioned about marriage and the life after, He replied, "Ye do err, not knowing the scriptures, *nor the power of God.* For in the resurrection they neither marry, nor are given in marriage, but are as angels in heaven" (Matthew 22:29-30 ASV, emphasis mine). What was Jesus referring to when He answered the question about marriage by saying "nor the power of God"? Could it be the hidden revelation that when two come together there is power, and marriage is just one expression of two things becoming one? Moreover, in that oneness the power of life is revealed by, for instance, producing children. This entire book is attempting to show that the nature of the receiver is necessary in order for the power of the giver to be manifested, just like in a marriage.

Can we admit that we are missing something? Are we willing to face our issues in our own hearts and homes before we attempt to come to the house of God or preach to the world? Let us not presume that we can teach others to be intimate with God while our own marriages are struggling in the area of deep, vulnerable intimacy.

What if we, as the bride, were poor in spirit with nothing to offer God? Would we then see His face? If we saw His face, would we then see His heart? If we saw His heart, would we feel His pain? If we felt His pain, would it cause us to rip open our calloused hearts and cry out to God? Are we willing to cry out to the only One able to heal and deliver us? What will it take for us to surrender our logical thinking and stop leaning on our own understanding that we acquired through the knowledge of good and evil? Will we wake up and see that, like the children of Israel wandering in the wilderness, we are not able to keep the commandments and that only God is good? If it were not for the pain of my marriage, I dare say I would never have awakened.

Chapter 2: She Is a Worm, But-Her-Fly

Over the years, I have heard the phrase *be true to yourself.* To be honest, my response was, "Of course I am true to myself. How could I be anything else?" In time I discovered that it was possible to *not* be true to myself. This is what happens when I become something other than myself to try to please others. I realized that I did this in order to feel protected, accepted, or loved.

In this chapter, I will show you how I came to *need* the approval of others and how I woke up to the fact that I was addicted to it. I was in such denial, I had no idea that I was seeking it or that others had failed to provide it. In my logic, I believed that I was deeply loved. I also loved as deeply as I possibly could with a broken heart. I wasn't even aware that I only felt loved when others approved of me and unloved if they didn't. After I got married, I unknowingly placed this responsibility on my husband as well. Being happily married was my dream. Everything I had ever read, watched, or sang declared that marriage was evidence of two people *in love*. Surely my marriage would make me feel complete. Isn't that the reason we get married in the first place?

I had no idea that marriage could not make me whole. Nor was I aware that I had become afraid of intimacy. In my fear of being rejected was hidden the illusion that if anyone got too close, they would discover how different I was and they would get rid of me. So behind my walls of self-protection I would stay until I found someone who would prove they loved me. This concept did not include the understanding that no human can complete another human. Only God can heal our broken hearts and make us whole. Only then would I even be free to experience intimacy with God first and then others.

As I look at my life objectively, I must admit that most of my life I have spent trying to get the approval of others. First, I **desired** to please my parents and grandparents. Then I sought the approval of my sisters. That grew into wanting the approval of friends, teachers, coaches, leaders, acquaintances, and even strangers. The problem with this endeavor is each of these people groups didn't all want the same thing. Therefore, I had become a groveling worm attempting to take on the shape of anyone who was willing to feed me their flattering words of what appeared to be approval. This kind of approval bore no fruit in my life. In fact, like a worm living in the dirt I was eating from the waste or droppings of anything or anyone who would throw me some kind of verbiage or action that had the appearance of approval.

This illusion was held in my emotional memories and affected every part of my life. It was like having a little leaven in a measure of flour. It will cause the entire loaf to be filled with yeast. This mentality secretly grew, filling my entire belief system, which affected every part of my life.

I was the classic mama's baby, over-achiever, teacher's pet, do-gooder, tattle-tale, super obedient, now-will-you-love-me kind of person. After I married, it continued. My house was so clean you could eat off my floors. Over the years, things changed as I went from one extreme to the other. You could still eat off of my floors: "What would you like? Popcorn, cereal, chips, chicken?" I became so sick of being everyone's slave that my pendulum swung to the other end of the spectrum; I was indifferent, angry, and independent.

For over twelve years, I tried to be the best wife and mother I could be. This was a noble goal, but my foundational beliefs that held me to this goal were sick and groveling. My soul was crying, "Love me, love me, would someone love me? Anybody, please love me!"

At the core, this was due to the belief that I was rejected. I did not feel in my heart that I belonged anywhere nor to anyone. How could this belief even be inside of me, much less at the core of my being? In my logic, I loved myself and I was surprised if anyone else didn't. However, the cycles in my life were cycles of loneliness and rejection.

I grew up the fifth of six girls. I was the only one who had fair skin and light hair. One of my earliest memories was being in a grocery store with my family. Someone stopped to talk to my mom as she was taken aback at the beauty of all these little dark-haired, dark-skinned, black-eyed little girls. She gazed at my sisters lovingly and asked, "Are *all* these little girls yours?" Years ago, in south Louisiana, there weren't many Mexican families around.

As a matter of fact, we were the only Mexican family I had ever seen except for my family in Arizona. My mother, however, had fair skin, blue eyes, and dark blonde hair.

After this lady admired my family and discovered all of these little beauties belonged to my mama, she turned to me and said, "Who is she?" My little heart sank as I received the message, "See, you don't fit!"

It is normal for kids to pick on each other, and being the baby for eight years I was no exception. I can remember being laughed at and told I was adopted. "Mama and Daddy are not your real parents. You were adopted. We found you in the garbage can and just felt sorry for you. See, you don't look like any of us." Now, before you take any offense, let's understand that this is just what kids do. Many kids pick on the weak. It is our human nature and the nature of pack animals. Though this may seem cruel, it is really pretty normal. I love my sisters and they love me. We are just like every other family. Not perfect, but perfect for each other.

Even though my dear mom comforted me and disciplined my sisters, making them apologize, my little heart was feeling rejected and unwanted. It wasn't long before it was settled in my limbic brain and heart-brain: "I do not fit anywhere, nor am I really loved. It must be true, for even my mother found pity on me." This belief had formed in my neural network before the age of four. It was one of my subconscious core beliefs—I was a groveling worm, I was rejected.

Please take note that this is the same thing as a conclusion, calculation, or a mark. Each time we have a wonder or ask the question why, our limbic and logical brain will cry out for an answer. If we wonder any question for 72 hours or longer, we will build a neurological vortex to receive the answer to the question. It is like an antenna that calls out to the entire universe, "Who, what, where, when, why, and how?"

The magnetic and electrical pulses from the heart-brain are very strong both magnetically and electrically. Our emotion-filled questions will attract an equal belief with something in it to fill the question or void with a conclusion. I call this an equal opposite. This is where Newton's Third Law is manifested in our thoughts, desires, and emotions. Let me be more specific to help you understand this invisible concept.

No Longer Dis-Eve'd

As this little girl under the age of five, I was developing my subconscious mold, which was formed by age seven. I would soon use my seven-year-old subconscious mold to filter and judge all my future experiences. I was now in a perpetual state of wondering, *How do I get acceptance?* I had already concluded that the following facts were my absolute truth.

- My skin was too white.
- My eyes were not dark enough.
- My hair was blonde, and therefore too light.
- I was the baby and, therefore, too little.
- I was Mama's favorite because she felt sorry for me.
- She rocked me and comforted me, so I must need pity.
- I had to find a way to get acceptance.
- But *how* was the question.

As I wondered, feeling sad and rejected, my body was keeping exact record of everything it saw, smelled, tasted, touched, and heard. In fact, it was creating something that scientists call a T-minus-one snapshot, a process in which our limbic brain and the body record our memories to protect us from similar circumstances in an effort to avoid pain or injury. They are electromagnetic, chemical recordings of all the facts, emotions, desires, and thoughts we experience; a recording of all of the five sensual experiences combined.

This is part of our survival system. It is from this system that the body determines if and when it will need any cortisol or adrenalin to fight or run. You may remember this is called our "fight or flight" instinct. It is needed if you were to face a lion or a bear. (That is, unless you are David the beloved in the Bible.) This is a really good thing that God created in us to help us survive. It can, however, work against us unless it is seen, understood, and then polished, thereby purging us from the need to run, hide, or fight. This must be transformed by God through the same pathway or memories that it was established in.

This instinct nature is also the same as the animal nature or the nature of a **beast**. What does Scripture say about this? "I said in mine heart concerning the estate of the sons of men, that God might *manifest* them, and that they might see that they themselves are **beasts**" (Ecclesiastes 3:18 KJV, emphasis mine). *Manifest,* here, means to clarify, show, examine, and make bright in order to clean, polish, purify, and purge out. Some translations say that God *tests* us to show us that we are like the beast. We did not need scientists to prove to us this truth written in the Bible, but it sure helps us to understand it.

Back to my little girl question: "How do I find acceptance to prove that I am loved?" This question could only be proposed from a position that assumed that I was in a state of rejection. This is equal to the statement, "I am not loved." My question was evidence that I did not feel loved. This was my foundational calculation or *belief* of who I was.

This process of calculating is seen in the Hebrew word *tephillâh.* Used in the Old Testament, it means intercession, supplication, hymn, and prayer; the root word is *pâlal.* This word means "to judge, to intreat, judgment, make prayer, and/or praying."

What did Jesus say about believing, praying, and receiving? "Therefore I say unto you, What things soever ye ***desire***, when ye ***pray***, ***believe*** that ye ***receive*** them, and ye shall have them" (Mark 11:24 KJV). This word "pray" in the New Testament is the Greek word *proseuchomai.* It comes from two words: *pros*[1] and *euchomai.*[2] It means "to pray to God, that is, supplicate, worship: pray earnestly for, make prayer, to wish, to will and indicating a forward movement in place, time and occasion with respect to a destination or end result or request."

Note that in order for us to know what we desire or will, we must be judging something. In fact, the word "desire" here in this text is the Greek word *aiteo,* and it means "to ask, beg, call for, crave, and require." It is compared to the word *punthanomai,* which means "to question and ascertain by inquiry" and implies to search for something. Moreover, it actually involves learning and understanding, which requires calculation and judgment. Without calculation and judgment, we can't be fully persuaded or have faith in the body. This is why we can believe in the logic and conscious brain, yet still have unbelief in the brain's limbic system, causing us to doubt.

Pay attention to the words that I've placed in bold italics. The English language will not provide us with a clear understanding and, therefore, will

---

1. Strongs G4314.
2. Strongs G2172.

leave us with the same results that we had yesterday. If I tell you what you already know, you will keep what you already have. I want to help you find the answer to the question, "I believe with my whole heart that God's Word is true, so why can't I get my prayers answered?" The reason is, we don't understand the words *pray* and *believe*.

Like I said, the very act of wondering created a new addition to my neural network in my brain and heart-brain. This network is established in layers of information that have been received from the time I was in the womb. Some of it was formed from my own mother's feelings that were recorded while her chemicals ran through my body. All of her T-minus-one snapshots that were formed by her pain passed though me in the form of emotional chemical ligands. This became part of my fight or flight limbic survival system—my subconscious mold. Moreover, I was formed from twenty-three chromosomes of each parent. Therefore, some of my network was passed on from my parents as well as from prior generations. This network then sent out that highly emotional question through magnetic and electric frequencies into the bio-magnetic field. This field is not bound by space or time. This is a field just like any other field. It is a place for seeds to be deposited and then return its fruit back to the one who released it. **This is prayer or supplication! It is already the *belief* that** "I must not be loved; therefore, I need to find love." My little soul was knocking, seeking, and asking. The problem with my condition at that time was my basic core belief—I am not loved—and that would hold me captive until I found true love. The problem was that I kept looking to other humans to find it. It was not until I was sick and tired of rejection that I was impelled to find the answers even if it cost me my entire life. I was now willing to die, and that is just what I did.

I can hear some of you asking, "Die? How?" That is a question that I take great joy in answering.

One year for my birthday, I proposed this question to Michael.

"Honey, you know this weekend is my birthday and we usually go out to eat. However, the Saints and LSU are having playoff games, and I know that you want to watch them. So, why don't I have dinner with my sisters and some friends and we can go out for my birthday next weekend? That way, we both can have what we want this weekend, but you and I can still celebrate my birthday after the games. Everyone will be happy."

He said, "Oh, no; I am happy to take you out for dinner."

"Really? You know you want to see the games. Baby, I promise, we can celebrate later. Once the games are over, they are over."

"No. I insist, I am taking you out."

"Okay, but we are not sitting in the bar to watch the game. I don't want to watch football on my date."

We arrived at the restaurant, and our daughter came with us. The waitress sat us in the dining room but, wouldn't you know it, right next to the bar in front of the big screen TVs. Ugh! Our food came and my daughter and I talked while Michael watched the game, only joining us for a second or two during the commercial breaks. Then, all of a sudden, we were shushed because we were distracting him. Oh, my goodness. I was so undone. My daughter and I sat silently to avoid a scene, but I was boiling. I decided in my heightened state of emotion, "never again."

My neural network from my past was beginning to crumble. Sorrow and suffering began to visit me often. It wasn't until years later that I understood just how much I needed to tear down the ancient foundations that had been established since I was seven years old.

Later, I asked Michael why he didn't take me up on my offer to stay at home and watch the game. We both knew that he wanted to. He explained that he didn't want to disappoint me and that he was even concerned that maybe I would retaliate later and throw it up at him to show him how he was failing at being a good husband. The truth is, these fears were valid.

For years, when he had failed to meet my expectations I would get my feelings hurt and he would ask me why I was hurting. I would customarily blame him for not making me feel loved. His heart was willing and loving. Our outside issues were not our real problems. They were hidden in both of our subconscious beliefs that were looking for some shred of evidence that we were good enough to be loved.

We then agreed that from then on we would be honest, even if it hurt. We were going to let our yes be yes and our no be no. I was finding my backbone and voice. He was starting to believe me when I said he was free to do what he really wanted to do. I had cut the strings, but now he was going to have to set out to see if I would use them as a whip or truly accept him as he was.

No Longer Dis-Eve'd

Not long after that episode, we were invited to a friend's birthday party. I accepted the invitation and couldn't wait to attend. These were some of my best friends and I loved hanging out with them and getting loud, laughing, and picking with healthy loving humor.

On the night of the party, I came home from work and started getting ready. Michael asked where I was going, and I told him to the birthday party.

"What? They didn't invite me?" Michael asked.

"Oh, no; they did, but I know you don't like it when I get loud and cut up, so I uninvited you."

"You can't uninvite me."

"Oh yes I can! Remember? We are going to be honest and I don't want you to come. If you come, you are going to want me to be quiet and just observe. I want to be loud and laugh loud. I want to be the life of the party at least once, and if time permits and everyone else has had a turn I am going to be the life of the party a second time. I am going to say blonde things by accident, and that will embarrass you. I don't want to embarrass you. I want to be myself, and that embarrasses you. If you go, I will not be able to be myself. I will have to be the 'Good Little Wife.' That is not the real me. I like the real me. At home, you like the real me, but when we get around other people, you want me to sit still and quiet. So, no, you can't come unless you drive your truck and go sit in the room with the men who will be watching the football game. You know that is what you really want to do anyway. Agreed?"

"Okay, agreed."

We went to the party and drove different vehicles. He hung out in the TV room with all of the men who wanted to watch the game, and I stayed in the kitchen dining area where the party was. I laughed loud, said blonde stuff, told corny jokes, and had the best time. Everyone liked the real me and so did I. Something in me was changing. The more I felt loved by Jesus, the less I needed others' approval. My old neural network was *dying*, and a new belief system was being established in my brain.

This process of discovering old lies about myself and having my heart crushed in the process seemed to have become a way of life for me. The unusual thing is, I was no longer afraid of sorrow nor suffering. God took His time and lovingly prepared me before He tore down my walls and their foundations. God would only take the tares out of my heart after the wheat was mature. Each time I would go through a deeper transition until I was fully persuaded in my emotions that God created me for Him to dwell in and that He took delight in dwelling with me on earth through my emotions.

There has never been a time when God requested me to face my fears that He did not deliver me.

In conclusion I learned, and hope to show you through our stories, that sorrow and suffering is the pathway to healing the subconscious brain. Here are two more Scriptures that reveal this same truth.

"Sorrow is better than laughter: for by the sadness of the countenance the heart is made *better*" (Ecclesiastes 7:3 KJV, emphasis mine). The word *better* in this text is the Hebrew word *yâtab*, and it means to (causatively) make well, *literally (sound, beautiful)* or figuratively (happy, successful, right): - be accepted, amend, use aright, benefit, be (make) better, seem best, make cheerful, be comely, + be content, diligent (-ly), dress, earnestly, find favour, give, be glad, do (be, make) good ([-ness]), be (make) merry, please (+ well), shew more [kindness], skilfully, X very small, surely, make sweet, thoroughly, tire, trim, very, be (can, deal, entreat, go, have) well [said, seen].

In order to understand these words, I sometimes look up each one to get the complete meaning of the word. I encourage you to do the same. I looked up the literal words for "sound" and "beautiful" italicized in bold above, and this is what I found.

"Sound" *tâmîym taw-meem* [3] From *Tamam*; entire (literally, figuratively or morally); also (as noun) integrity, truth: - **without blemish, complete**, full, perfect, sincerely (-ity), sound, **without spot**, undefiled, upright (-ly), whole.[4] *Tamam* means a primitive root; to complete, in a good or a bad sense, literally or figuratively, transitively or intransitively: - accomplish, cease, be clean [pass-] ed, consume, have done, (come to an, make an) end, fail, come to the full, be all gone, X be all here, be (make) perfect, be spent, sum, be (shew self) upright, be wasted, whole.

---

3. Strongs, H8549..

4. Strongs, H8552.

"Beautiful" is made up of two words, *yapheh* and *toar*: beautiful, fair, fairest one, goodly, pleasant, well, to be bright, beautiful countenance, favored; and it goes even deeper.

Let's stop here with the word study. Please forgive my in-depth definitions here, but I wanted to show you that in order to truly know the meaning, we need to know the words and where they came from.

"Remembering mine affliction and my misery, the wormwood and the gall. My soul hath them still in remembrance, and is humbled in me. This I recall to my *mind,* therefore have I hope. It is of the Lord's mercies that we are not consumed, because his compassions fail not" (Lamentations 3:19-22 KJV). This Hebrew word for *mind* in this text is *lêb,* and it means "the heart" (Strong's H3820).

We are not able to love with all of our hearts until our hearts believe that they are loved in and through the emotions. Once the heart feels loved and the new subconscious is established and is whole, nothing is missing nor broken. That is why Jesus told us to seek the kingdom first and then everything would be added, and everything really means everything.

The truth and science of this chapter show us that God is not mocked, and when we sow our heartfelt beliefs into this bio-magnetic field (the atmosphere), we reap what our hearts hold to be true, even if our hearts are believing a lie. As a little girl, I believed I was rejected and I created my own reality in cycles of rejection. However, when I saw in my emotions that I am loved and it is not possible to earn love, my old neural network *died* and a new one now lives in me. My new network feels like a daughter of the Most High, the bride of Jesus. This belief system is creating my current reality, which is filled with abundance and joy while living on the edge of my seat. Once I lived as a groveling worm, feeding on dust, who discovered I was bound and hanging by a thread of existence. Then, when I could live that way no longer, I fought my way through my sorrow and found my wings of freedom. Yes, I had been living life as a codependent person who groveled like a worm, a ButHerFly: but I had found my true self in Jesus, no longer needing the approval of others. It was truly like finding my wings and flying. That is why you will hear me say, "She is a worm, ButHerFly."

Chapter 3: The Brutal Truth

How did I end up in that spiritual coma discussed in chapter one? I was sick and tired of Michael not complying with my idea of a godly man. Being his "Holy Spirit" was too heavy and I was exhausted. I was still in love with Michael, but I could now feel that I was becoming indifferent to his criticism and attempts to control me. In fact, when I tried to tell him over and over again that he was doing this, he could not see it. He was completely blind to what I was talking about. After all, he was a really good husband. I had told him so, and his good deeds, integrity, and godliness also testified of his efforts. Moreover, he loved me with all that he had. Both of us were broken and empty, thinking that we could heal and fill each other.

We both agreed that we had dysfunctional behavior, but on the surface it looked like we were handling it pretty well. We were facing our issues, asking for forgiveness and attempting to accept each other's apologies. We talked and listened the best we could. We even parroted back what we were saying to each other, using the speaking and listening skills that God had given us. We were both pretty secure in our roles outwardly and life seemed pretty darn good. Michael worked for the government and I ran my mortgage business. I ministered once a month by holding women's retreats, and we attended church regularly. We were the model family. We had two amazing, smart, kind, and well-behaved children. Both were on the honor roll in a Christian school and they were well-liked. As parents, when we hurt our children's feelings, we were swift to restore their tender hearts, and yet we were biblically strict so as to not spoil them. Michael and I didn't realize there were things deep in our hearts that were killing our passion for each other.

Everything looked amazing, and we were doing all the right things. We even counseled other couples, and they were well pleased with the results. So why was I vacillating in and out of a relational coma?

No Longer Dis-Eve'd

One evening after Michael and I made love, I retreated into the bathroom for a long bath, while Michael relaxed in front of the television to watch the game. As I sat in the tub, I began to weep. I couldn't understand what I was feeling or why.

I began to pray and God asked me, "What are you feeling?"

"Dirty," I replied, "but I don't know why."

"It is because you did not make love to Michael tonight; you had sex with him."

"What! That's not true, God! He pleased me and he always loves me with care and passion. He is an amazing lover."

"Yes, he did make love to you, but you did not make love to him. You accepted his invitation because you did not want to hurt his feelings and make him feel rejected. Your heart is wounded and your hearts are not one. Michael thinks everything is okay, but you have unforgiveness toward him. That is why you are feeling dirty. Fornication always feels dirty."

"But we are married; how is that fornication?"

"Your marriage certificate does not certify your love for each other; your hearts do. Your heart is shut down because you feel he can't listen and he refuses to learn any new communication skills. So, you were just going through the motions to avoid another confrontation. You need to go and apologize to him."

"Me apologize? But he is the one who refuses to deal with our heart issues. I can't make him. I have tried everything I know, but nothing works."

"Are you ready to let Me work in this situation, or would you like to continue as his god? I have seen your application for the co-Holy Ghost position, but honestly, there are no openings at this time. However, I am sure as soon as my Holy Spirit needs help, we will let you know."

Deflated, I replied, "What do I do next?"

"First go apologize and tell him about what happened in here just now. Tell him that you fornicated with him and that I told you it would destroy the marriage if you continued and that you were not able to do that again. Ask him to separate your bed for prayer and fasting. Ask him to sleep upstairs, and if he will not, then you sleep up there."

"But he will freak out. What if he says no or leaves me?"

"What if you do nothing and your love dies? What will you do if you keep this up until your skin crawls?"

"Oh no, God. I have seen many Christian women who ignore their hearts until their love dies, and after their skin begins to crawl, the marriage is over. I can't stand the thought of that happening. Okay, I will tell him. Please help me."

"I am helping you, My daughter. I am putting My words in your mouth."

God reminded me of a promise He had made to me in my first year of marriage. I thought He had forgotten. But He assured me that He had not. He was waiting for me to be fully persuaded that nothing and no one but God could deliver me from my cycles of sin and death. What was this promise? You may ask.

Only weeks into our marriage, Michael's high school ex-girlfriend began sending him letters and calling our home and hanging up as soon as I would answer. I cried out to God and He said, "Don't fight her. You take care of her heart and I will take care of your marriage. I did not die for your marriage; I died for her soul." I fought God for nine weeks straight while my pastor taught on the story of Jonah. He did not want to go to Nineveh, and I did not want to show the love of Jesus to Michael's ex.

One morning, our pastor said, "Would someone listen to God, I am tired of preaching on Jonah!"

After returning home from church, I fell on my face weeping. I cried out, "Okay God, if You will love her through me, then I am willing, but if You don't, I can't!" Through what I can only describe as a miracle, I was flooded with love for her as I lay on the floor weeping. She soon accepted Jesus as her Lord and Savior and we became friends. In fact, I went to see her only minutes after her father died. She told me a lot about her life and that no one had ever loved her like I did. "I see the love of God in your eyes, and that makes all the difference in the world to me." Only God could manifest such a love in my heart.

Back to the request of God to tell my husband the truth about my heart being shut down while making love and asking him to forgive me. It was time for brutal truth and no more blaming him for my issues.

No Longer Dis-Eve'd

I went into the living room with tears and trembling. I had no idea what Michael would say or how he would react to what I was about to tell him. More than anything, I dreaded the pain I was about to cause him. This kind of truth is brutal, and to be truthful I was terrified of it.

He was devastated. The pain and anger in him was sharp and pungent, yet humility and shame covered his face. I could see the disappointment in his eyes as he faced the feeling of my accusations and his fear of failure. He struggled to understand and asked lots of questions. Sobbing, I dug deep and told him the entire truth, admitting that we had not made love, but in fact my heart was shut down and I did not want to hurt his feelings by denying him. I had taken responsibility for my codependency and was no longer willing to beg for approval. It was time to face our issues and use my voice to speak the truth in love. I was no longer willing to be controlled by fear and manipulation. You see, in order for me to remain a victim, I needed a bully: and Michael had been bullying me for years. I had blamed him for treating me with disrespect and emotional abuse, but in order for our marriage to heal, I had to take responsibility for my part. The only way he could bully me was if I was willing to remain his victim. God was showing me how to face my own truth and my own issues. I was sick and tired of being a victim. Without my relationship with God, I would have been to afraid to face our issues: first by dealing with my own, and then confronting him with his.

He asked why I didn't tell him before, and I said, "I did tell you. Each time I tried to explain my heart, and how I could no longer endure your endless anger and your verbal and emotional abuse, you would tell me that I was beating a dead horse and then apologize for the last outburst. I would forgive you only to repeat the same cycles over and over again. I just can't take going through all of the motions with no heart change."

He agreed to sleep upstairs, and each day we both would lay prostrate before God seeking for mercy and help as our hearts cried out with deep sorrow. Neither one of us knew the other person was doing the same thing. It was not until we talked each night that we discovered that God was speaking the same thing to each of us. It was truly remarkable. He was starting to see that all that he had judged me for he was doing to God, and I was learning the same thing. We both began to take responsibility for our own cycles of judging and becoming. We had recently started studying about judgement, as Jesus taught in chapter seven of the book of Matthew. The Holy Spirit came to reveal righteousness, judgment, and sin, and this revelation about judgment was breaking our hearts and bringing us to our knees.

During this time, we had agreed, at the direction of the Holy Spirit, for Michael to refrain from touching me in any sexual way. I explained what happens when love dies and the skin experiences the crawling sensation. His touch had never produced that feeling, and we both were fearful that if he did touch me prior to our hearts healing, it might happen. Knowing this, we agreed it would be best for him to hold me as if I were a broken child. In fact, we both were and didn't realize it. God was about to show us just how broken we both really were.

We set very clear boundaries to protect each other's hearts. We agreed to only kiss on the forehead, cheek, or hand. He held me in his arms, careful to not touch my breast, waist, or below the belt. If he did touch my legs, it would only be on the outer thigh. Michael was amazing. He not only agreed, but only advanced within these guidelines after asking and confirming with me that my heart was okay. He was so tender and loving.

"I will wait for you forever," he said.

The tears in his eyes were hard to look at in the beginning, so we often cried together in the dark.Each night, we would tuck the children into bed. They were aware that Daddy was sleeping upstairs. We had informed them that we were praying and fasting, seeking God for our family. They were allowed to ask us questions and we answered appropriately for their ages. Not once were they afraid we would divorce, and they were actually glad to know that we were dealing with our issues. Kids are a lot more aware sometimes than adults are.

God had instructed me to not kiss Michael on the lips until our hearts mended. As soon as God spoke this to me, I began to feel a large lump in my throat. It felt like that feeling you get when you are holding back your tears and have the urge to swallow hard. The weird thing is, I didn't need to cry, and it stayed in my throat twenty-four seven.

I asked God, "What is this lump, and should I go to the doctor?"

"No," He replied. "This is Me. I will make it rest when it is safe for you to kiss Michael. Two hearts co-mingled in unity are expressed in words first, then in the emotions, and then are celebrated in the kiss. When you kiss him before your hearts are united, that will dishonor both of your hearts. If you listen closely to your hearts, you will know when to kiss. In fact, your heart will impel you to kiss, and that is true passion. I made you this way. Father, Holy Spirit, and I all are moved with compassion. We wait for it, as we are moved by the union of our nature. This is the nature of love."

God did not tell us how long to stay in separate beds, and, in fact, we were wondering how long it would last.

When I asked God why this was even needed, He explained, "When a man makes love to his wife and she is consensual, he concludes logically that whatever problems existed are now over and that you have both moved on."

I was in shock, because this is not what I felt at all.

I replied, "God, are You kidding me? He doesn't realize that I am only coming back together with him in lovemaking to show my willingness to trust him again?"

"No; go ask him."

I did just that. To my surprise, Michael confirmed that I had heard God correctly.

He replied, "Well yeah!"

"Oh, no! I am not saying that at all. I am saying, 'Here, take me in your arms again. I trust you with all of me. Please don't break my heart again.' No wonder God had instructed us to separate the marriage bed."

Remember in the Scriptures where Paul offers us instructions on how to deal with someone who claims to be in Christ yet persists in various types of sin. He explains how we are not even allowed to eat dinner with them. How is it that I could understand that I should not eat with a person with whom I had division due to persistent sin, but I could not understand why having sexual union when my heart is not in union will destroy the relationship? This too was persistent sin. I was living a sin in the most holy union of lovemaking by concealing my heart and allowing my husband to believe a lie. Men and women definitely do not see the world the same way. We need the wisdom of God to navigate this union called marriage.

Three weeks passed and our hearts were beginning to overflow with validation, honor, respect, and love. We were looking into each other's eyes when that lump in my throat rested.

I heard the Holy Spirit say, "Now your hearts are one, and that is a true kiss. You are moving in the spirit of love. You can kiss him now."

I leaned in to kiss his lips when Michael gently stopped me. He touched my lips with his finger and said, "Are you sure? I will wait forever for you."

"Yes," I said.

Tears flowed down my face as we embraced in a kiss of passion. As you can imagine, that night we rejoined our marriage bed, for our hearts were reunited in love.

God had done in three weeks what we had tried to accomplish for the prior nineteen years. God is not looking for people to volunteer to help Him. On the contrary, He wants His equal opposite.

How are we the equal opposite of Jesus? We are the ones who have no light of our own and need Him to fill our darkness. We were created by God in the flesh, who are being transformed by Christ's Spirit into the sons of God. One day we will put on a body like the one Jesus had after His resurrection. Jesus is God, who is Spirit, who came to earth in the form of a man. We are humans, who will leave the form of flesh and put on a form like unto Jesus after His resurrection. Our dominant nature starts out as flesh and His dominant nature was and remains Spirit. We are weak and He alone is strong. So, what is the equal part? We are the dwelling place of God the Father and God the Holy Spirit, and in Christ we are one. That is also the definition of equal. This is the marriage union. The two in one body rolled together. Christ in us, and us in Him.

Jesus wants a bride with whom He can make His strength known in her weakness. A receiver to give His word—His seed—to. Now can you see the allegory taking shape? A husband takes joy in providing for and protecting his bride physically, as well as guarding her honor. Because God is the "I Am," I can happily be the "I Am Not."

"And Enoch walked with God: and he was not; for God took him" (Genesis 5:24 KJV). This word *took* (*lâqach*) means that God "accepted, carried, in folded with, to be rolled together with, mingled with, received, reserved, seized, sent for, to take away, to win" Enoch (Strong's H3947).

In the Song of Solomon, the Lover beckons her, "*Come*, my beloved, let us go forth into the field; let us lodge in the villages. Let us get up early to the vineyards; let us see if the vine flourish, whether the tender grape appear, and the pomegranates bud forth: there will I give thee my loves" (Song of Solomon 7:11-12 KJV emphasis mine).

Moreover, the woman in Proverbs 31 considers a field and *buys* it with the fruit of her hands. This is talking about the field of her heart. It is describing her fruitfulness that is birthed from her heart and as a result of their union. It is the fruit of the spiritual union with Jesus her groom. The word meaning behind *come* my beloved is to walk with me alongside, be weak, and whirl with Him. When she considers and *buys* the field, it is the same Hebrew word as when God *took* Enoch. Hidden in these beautiful allegories is the spiritual union where man and God become one. It reveals mankind as the weaker vessel whirling together—God in man and man in God. It is where the weaker is filled to overflowing by the stronger. What a beautiful picture and mystery of His union with us, in us, and through us.

Jesus finds great pleasure in making Himself manifest in us. Are we ready to surrender as the weaker vessel and watch Jesus show Himself strong? If a man knew how, he would find great satisfaction in cherishing his wife's heart just like Jesus does the heart of His bride; he too would die to experience this kind of passionate union.

With all of this being true, a man does not want a woman so weak that she is a pushover or a whining, codependent baby. He wants a receiver who desires and is able to give back unto him, while remaining open to receive all of his heart. Moreover, she lovingly and firmly requires him to honor her as well.

A wife is designed to give her husband children, a place in her heart he can trust, her body to join with his, and her time. He also, whether he knows it or not, wants a woman who will hold him at his word and require it of him.

Because of her strength, she is not smothering and is content being together or apart. Her strength comes from within, and she will help him to find his inner strength as well.

Let's not take it too far, ladies, for no man wants to be treated like a helpless worm either. Have you ever helped your husband drive from the passenger seat of your automobile? Do they really need our help? How weak must a man be to need the assistance of his wife in order to drive the car? It is a wonder he has ever made it to the store and back. Does a man look for a bride who can show him just how weak he is? I think not. This is crazy, yet we as women do this every day.

The marriage between mankind and Jesus is just like this. Jesus is our shield and strong tower, yet we think He needs our help. Moreover, God tells us to hold Him at His word. God does not want us to be a pushover or a bully. Nor does He teach us to be ruled by others, by religion, by systems, or by fear. He desires to make us hunger and thirst for Him and then fill us to overflowing.

He delights in those times when we are not able to see Him in the darkest moments of our lives, yet we remain at rest in the beauty of His unending love that refuses to separate from us. Why? Jesus takes joy in filling us with His Spirit and the Word of Truth. Didn't He teach only the poor in spirit shall see God? The bride understands her darkness yet knows she is beautiful in His eyes; that is what makes her lovely. This understanding is her humility and her strength. It is in not trusting herself that she rests in Him alone.

This is what it means to be a living soul. It indicates one whose nature receives because it is empty. Like the earth that he was made from, Adam was without form and void. He was blood and mud fashioned in the image of God, both male and female—male as the giver and female as the receiver. God was the giver in creation and Adam was the receiver. The male nature revealed the glory of God as the giver, and Eve revealed the glory of God as the receiver, who multiplies the seed only to return it to her giver.

There is a beautiful balance that is ever changing between that which is measured and that which cannot be measured. This is the nature of humans—measurable dust and immeasurable breath. We are called "human." Hue is tint or color. It is the refraction or dividing of light that allows us to see color. Likewise, when God divided Adam into man and woman, it was so that the full nature could be seen. Dividing reveals, magnifies, and multiplies. Therefore, division is a good thing. God gave this to us as a gift. Seeing it as bad sets us up to judge God. As a matter of fact, God said it was very good when man was divided and woman was revealed.

Likewise, the division that was manifesting in our marriage was not bad. In fact, it was the very thing needed to open our eyes and see God's love toward us and to see the mystery of the marriage.

Our fallen nature caused us to be exhausted and weary. Only after I felt hopeless and sinking into a spiritual coma was I able to not trust in my own nature.

Why would God tell us to put off this nature if He said it was very good? What are we missing in our understanding about our nature? Ephesians tells us to put off the *old man*. I can't take off my flesh and hang it in my closet. How can I put off what I don't understand; how can I put off my dust nature? So, what is Paul saying?

In the Greek and Hebrew, to "put off" means "completion, to complete the departure, a reversal." In the beginning mankind, deceived by the serpent (learned experiences), ate from the tree and departed from God. In the fullness of time Christ came to restore us to the Father. It is this return that completes the departure. In fact, the third letter of the Hebrew alphabet is *Gimel*. It looks like a high-heeled shoe and means "to run away in order to return." Another way to express its meaning is "to nurse in order to wean." It is loving for a parent to wean a child and help it to mature or become complete. Something is complete only when its fullness is revealed. For example, the fullness of the male cannot be seen without the female. It is only when the female gives birth to the seed of her husband that her husband's full nature can be understood as a father. It is in his child that the full understanding of his seed is revealed. In fact, he gave his seed away in order for it to return.

The bride of man started the departure, and the bride of Christ shall complete the departure, which is to return. Moreover, to put off means the opposite of stand; it means to lie horizontal or prostrate. To lie prostrate can mean to be humble and bow down before our King Jesus spiritually. Moreover, to lie prostrate is also where we get the word *conceive*—"to rest, to purpose, to be settled, to bow or bend."

The position of a woman who is receiving a seed from her husband is the physical position that reveals the natural flesh union. It is this union of flesh that reveals the spiritual union. This is how we perceive not the things we can see, but rather realities we cannot see. To be the bride of Christ is to bow our spirits and our hearts, in death to our own ways, and lie prostrate with godly sorrow, broken in repentance as we seek to know the heart of God. It is in this broken and contrite state that He makes known His secrets to us and puts His revelatory Word into our hearts. Only the living Word can complete us and make us whole. Now we can see how the word complete is the same as the word bride, for without a bride, a man's full nature cannot be experienced; likewise, the bride is complete as we, the members, rest together as one and in one body with Jesus being the head.

When Michael and I were helpless and lying prostrate before God, he spoke into us and healed our hearts. God was in fact completing us by showing us how to not trust in our works, our intellect, or self-protection.

Like the soil, we were learning to be at rest, knowing that we could do nothing. Humans, like soil, are at rest and are complete in our nature to be a receiver of the seed from the farmer/husband. To put off the old man is to be the receiver and not the giver. In other words, wake up and understand and take on the position of a bride.

In the Song of Solomon, we read that the woman is dark, which also means void.

Her lover's reply in rebuttal is, "Yes, but lovely."

Her nature of being a receiver is lovely. For without her, he could not make the fullness of his nature known by giving his seed and then her yielding him a son or daughter.

Before Jesus died on the cross, He cried out, "It is finished." He was actually saying *it is complete.* Again, this is the same word as "put off." Jesus was completing us and we Him.

There is a promise spoken of in the book of Hebrews that says it is still waiting to be *fulfilled or completed.* This is the promise or oath to enter into the *rest of God. Rest* is a word that is revealed in multiple ways. Let's look deeper into the word to see the mystery as it is now being revealed.

- **Rested**/shabath: to **repose**, desist, make to, cease, celebrate, cause to make fail, suffer to be lacking, leave, put away, put down, make to rest, rid, still, take away.

- **Rest**/manoach: quiet, **"settled"** spot, home, place of rest, to dwell, stay, let fall, give comfort, lay, remain, give rest, make rest, have rest, cause to be at rest, to set down. Mnuchah to **repose** peacefully, consolation, **matrimony**, concretely abide, comfortable, ease, quiet, resting place, still. Manoach: a settled spot, a home, a place of rest, to dwell.

- **Rest**/yathar: to exceed, to excel, to remain, be left, to leave, cause to abound, to preserve, to leave a remnant, to make plenteous, to preserve, the remainder, the residue, the **"rest."**
- **Ended**/kalah: to end, ceased, finished, perish, **"complete,"** prepare, consume, accomplish, destroy utterly, expire, fail, faint, finish, fulfil, have, bring to pass, wholly reap, make clean, waste.
- **Bride**/kallah: a son's wife, a daughter-in-law, spouse, from the word kalal, **to be "complete."**
- **Elsabeth**/Elsabet: from elysheba: God of the oath. It comes from the words, el, sheba shib ah, sgaba, and together they mean *The oath of God "complete,"* to seven oneself, to fill, to satisfy. Moreover, they mean strength as a ram, rolled together by twisting the body as in copulation. The promise of the rest of God, completed.
- **Finished**/tamam: **to** *"complete,"* accomplish, cease, be clean, consume, have done, end, fail, come to the full, be all gone, be all here, be or make perfect, be spent, sum, shew self, upright, be wasted, be whole.
- **Seven**/shaba: to seven oneself, that is to swear as if by repeating a declaration seven times. An adjure, a charge, an oath, with an oath, feed to the full, to take an oath straitly, to fill to satisfaction, to suffice, to **"fulfil."** [5]

It is important to look at all of these words to get a deeper revelation of the words *rest* and *complete*. We are instructed by God to remember the Sabbath to keep it holy. If we don't understand the word, it is not possible to understand that the promised condition that the bride would eventually find herself in is "The Rest of God." Rest is the promised perfection of His love manifesting in us. Can you see how rest is to God and how it correlates to the words *complete, bride, Sabbath, seventh, ended, finished,* and *Elsabeth?* Is it becoming clear that in order for the two in a marriage to rest, they must be

---

5. See Strongs See H7650, H7651.

complete in who they are before they can rest in the union of marriage? On the cross Jesus declared it is finished. He was at the climax of His suffering when he cried this word. He was proclaiming His bride in this very word. Moreover, He was declaring her rest in Him by way of promise.

The crown on Jesus' head and the words "it is finished" were symbols of completion and rest. He declared the *completion* of the cursed soil that started when Adam and Eve relied on the knowledge of good and evil. By speaking this word and wearing a crown of **thorns**, He was saying, "My bride is complete when she rests as we suffer and share the same sorrow, trusting that I came in the flesh to know and understand her suffering heart." Only then can we rest in Him, which is the same as to reign with Him. It is this revelation that causes us to awaken and count it a joy to suffer with Christ. Moreover, this causes us to not see it as an area in our lives where the Devil has attacked us or an area where we were reaping some kind of punishment for our past behaviors. Were you aware that the word *curse* (*qalal*) means, "to be light, to make light, to be swift, small, sharp, easy, trifling, vile, abate, make bright, to bring into contempt, to despise, ease, to set light, to afflict, to esteem, to make vile, to point, to pierce, to inculcate, sharp, to teach diligently"? This brings clarity to the reason Jesus had to suffer the curse of the tree to complete the process of bringing all things to the light or to make them complete.

The seventh day of the week was the final decree of God that His promised rest would not go unfulfilled. It is in the word Sabbath that the promise of completion or the bride is hidden. Look at the words Sabbath and Elizabeth and how they both mean the promised daughter of oath or the promised rest/completion. This is the mystery of the Sabbath and is also the mysteries of the bride. Mysteries are hidden throughout the Old and New Testament; who will search them out? Only a king, that's who. "It is the glory of God to conceal a thing: but the honour of kings is to search out a matter" (Proverbs 25:2 KJV). Note the word *king* in this text means "to reign, to ascend the throne, to induct into royalty, to take counsel, to consult, to be king, to make queen, to begin to reign, to rule." [6]

---

6. Strong's H4428.

No Longer Dis-Eve'd

First woman was concealed by God on the inside of Adam. If woman were not taken out of man, then the nature of man could not manifest. Therefore, the actual nature of a woman shines the light on the nature of a man, and the nature of man shines the light on the nature of God. The Old Testament says a worthy woman is called a crown to her husband, and in the New Testament she is called the glory of her husband.

An honorable bride is the glory of her husband for she brings about understanding, uncovers, accounts, calculates, makes visibly understood, brings about rest. Rest can only be experienced when love is conceived in the heart. I was taught that I had to have faith that God loved me and believe it with all of my heart. Moreover, I was taught that I could not trust my feelings but had to have faith. Faith means fully persuaded, not to try to have a big, bigger, or biggest amount of faith. Before we move on into the next chapter, let's understand how the emotional part of us, which is the female part of us, works. Emotions are unseen and appear as dark, but oh, they are so lovely.

Are you aware that part of our brain is emotional and part of it is logical? They represent the male and female. Knowledge being the expression of the divine father and emotions being the expression of the divine mother.

They are very different and reside in different parts of the brain. The primitive brain is called the limbic or diencephalon and resides on both sides of the thalamus. It supports emotion, behavior, motivation, long-term memory, and the sense of smell. It is in this part of the brain where most of the emotional memory is housed in something called the amygdala. It is also primarily responsible for the formation of new memories. These types of memories are not created without the emotion and are directly connected to the heart-brain matter that resides in the heart.

The heart has forty thousand neurites that make up the heart-brain. These two, the limbic and the heart-brain, function as one unit. This part of the brain is responsible for the homeostasis in the body, which includes the regulation of body temperature; the pH balance of the bodily fluids; the concentration of sodium, potassium, and calcium; as well as the sugar in our blood. It does this despite our dietary intake, our environment, or our actions. It is these bodily functions that maintain the life of the person. Its primary function is to keep the body in a state of rest/peace.

The frontal lobe, on the other hand, contains most of the dopamine sensitive neurons and is associated with reward, attention, short-term memory, task, planning, and motivation.

Both parts of the brain calculate and affect one another. The limbic would be considered the emotional brain and the frontal lobe would be the logical brain. It has recently been discovered that the magnetic charge in the emotions/limbic brain is 5,000 times stronger than the magnetic charge in the intellectual/logical brain. Moreover, the electric charge in the emotions/limbic is 100 times stronger than the intellectual/logical brain. Therefore, if we believe in our logical brain 100 percent while at the same time having doubt in our emotional brain, which is connected to and is also part of the heart, the heart will override the logical brain. You can deny your feelings, but you will stay double minded. It is not possible for the logical brain to overpower the emotions. It may be able to diminish the emotions temporarily, but it will not manifest as whole or complete. It will thirst again.

When our logic believes different than our limbic, it is called a double mind. We do not have heart coherence or peace in this state. In times past I was taught that I had to control my feelings and not trust them. This is not actually possible. Our body responds in spite of our logic to what we feel in our emotions. This is because our subconscious is formed by the emotional memories held both in the heart and the limbic. This explains why a person who is no longer on the battlefield of Vietnam cannot logically override his emotions. It is impossible to believe with all of your heart, mind, and soul if your feelings are not in agreement. In other words, you believe what you feel, no matter what your brain tells you. No amount of logic can still the panic of the veteran's heart because the heart is 5,000 times stronger magnetically and 100 times stronger electronically.

Our knowledge of good and evil has ruled us long enough. Now is the time to accept our call as the bride and birth the manifested Word of God. In so doing we shall see the manifested power of God with signs and wonders like the world has never seen. Jesus called it greater works. Only Jesus can re-Eve all (reveal). The devil dis-Eve'd (deceived) us. Now is the time to Re-see Eve (receive) the truth of who we are. It is our identity that we lost when we trusted in ourselves as those who can discern good from evil, turning us into judges or little gods. Let us remain like the soil (with no light of our own) and marry our farmer. We are the body, the branch, the heart, the soil, the receiver, the lamp with no light of our own. (Re See Eve, "The Her.")

No Longer Dis-Eve'd is obviously a play on words. I hope that I have sparked an interest in your heart to study not only words but the Hebrew alphabet as well, where God has hidden mysteries in plain sight. Some may say that this kind of play on words may work in the English but not in other languages. I suggest you try it out, as I have. Before God scattered the languages of mankind, we were all of one language. It is reasonable to hypothesize that they all hold a part of each other. I hope you take some joy in this small taste of how words and seeds truly hold within them much more than meets the eye.

Can we learn more about ourselves as mankind by looking at the word *Eve*? What does it mean that Eve is the mother of all living? Everything that is living came from a dark place, or we could say a place of mystery. God "hides or conceals a matter," but a king will search it out or bring it forth. This is the same as to give birth to it. Seeds are hidden in the darkness of the soil. Babies are hidden in the darkness of the womb. Even the word *heaven* means out of our understanding or comprehension. Heaven is eternal and without measurement or understanding. Notice how we call the time when the sun goes down "evening." The word *evening* contains the word Eve. Evening means "covering, dusk, night." Notice it is in the darkness of the night that we rest. True rest is the ability to remain in a place of not trusting in our own understanding, knowing that God's love is keeping us in all things and at all times.

Everything that is living comes from the hidden/dark. Even Moses had to go talk to God in the "dark clouds." Allegorically, to remain in a place of not trusting in our own understanding is to allow the Word of God to be inside of us without understanding and allowing the Holy Spirit to cause the Word of God to sprout forth from within our lack of understanding. It is in this manner that we are the bride birthing forth the living Word. This is who we are called to be in the earth. We are the manifested sons of God that the earth is groaning with and for. It is groaning for us to be unveiled. It is our calling to be the one void of knowing, and holding the position of the weaker vessel as the receiver of the Word, God's seed, and God's understanding. It is in revelation that it the Word might be multiplied and shine out of us like a beacon of light to a lost and dying world. For we are the branches and He is the Vine. The branch is where the flower blooms and brings forth the fruit. A plant is both in the darkness of the earth and in the light of the sun, in the open air or heavens. Likewise, so are we: dark, yet lovely, knowing nothing, yet filled with the Truth.

Take note of the words below and see how the word "life," "sprout," and "pierced" are all related and reveal different measures of the same truth. Life is a mystery and its source is not seen. It is out of darkness that Jesus calls us all into His marvelous light.

- H2332: *chavvâh khav-vaw'* Causative from H2331; lifegiver; *Chavvah* (or Eve), the first woman: - Eve.

- H2331: *châvâh khaw-vah'* A primitive root; (compare H2324 to show, H2421); properly to live; by implication (intensively) to declare or show: - show.

- H2324: *chăvâ' khav-aw'* to show

- H2421: *châyâh khaw-yaw'* A prim root (compare H2331, H2424); to live, whether literally or figuratively; causatively to revive: - keep (leave, make) alive, X certainly, give (promise) life, (let, suffer to) live, nourish up, preserve (alive), quicken, recover, repair, restore (to life), revive, (X God) save (alive, life, lives), X surely, be whole.

- H2416: *chay khah'ee* From H2421; alive; hence raw (flesh); fresh (plant, water, year), strong; also (as noun, especially in the feminine singular and masculine plural) life (or living thing), whether literally or figuratively: - + age, alive, appetite, (wild) beast, company, congregation, life (-time), live (-ly), living (creature, thing), maintenance, + merry, multitude, + (be) old, quick, raw, running, springing, troop.

- H2498: *châlaph khaw-laf'* A primitive root; properly to slide by, that is, (by implication) to hasten away, pass on, spring up, pierce or change: - abolish, alter change, cut off, go on forward, grow up, be over, pass (away, on, through), renew, sprout, strike through.

- H3127: *yôneqeth yo-neh'-keth* Feminine of H3126; a sprout: - (tender) branch, young twig.

- H3126: *yônêq yo-nake'* Active participle of H3243; a sucker; hence a twig (of a tree felled and sprouting): - tender plant.

- H3243: *yânaq yaw-nak'* A primitive root; to suck; causatively to give milk: - milch, nurse (-ing mother), give, make to) suck (-ing child, -ling).

- H3187: *yâchaś yaw-khas'* A primitive root; to sprout; used only as denominative from H3188; to enroll by pedigree: - (number after, number throughout the) genealogy (to be reckoned), be reckoned by genealogies.

- H3188: *yachaś yakh'*-as From H3187; a pedigree or family list (as growing spontaneously): - genealogy.

- H6779: *tsâmach tsaw-makh'* A primitive root; to sprout (transitively or intransitively, literally or figuratively): - bear, bring forth, (cause to, make to) bud (forth), (cause to, make to) grow (again, up), (cause to) spring (forth, up).

- H6780: *tsemach tseh'-makh* From H6779; a sprout (usually concretely), literally or figuratively: - branch, bud, that which (where) grew (upon), spring (-ing).

- G2073: *hespera hes-per'-ah* Feminine of an adjective ἐσπερός hesperos (evening); the eve (G5610 being implied): - evening (-tide).

Are you ready to receive your identity back? Let us no longer be "dis Eve'd." Let us rise and shine for the morning is come.

"And Jesus said unto him, The foxes have holes, and the birds of the heaven have nests; but the Son of man hath not where to lay his head" (Luke 9:58 ASV).

Will you be the bride on whom Jesus can rest His head? Will you be the receiver heart where Jesus can put His word? Will you surrender your trust in the knowledge of your past experiences and just rest in having the nature of soil? This is the nature of a bride. The whole earth is waiting for us to be unveiled and manifest in the greater works. Jesus was called a prophet "*of*" Nazareth, not "*from*" Nazareth. And Nazareth means "The Branch." This means that Jesus came to prophesy into existence His bride. He prophesied "of" the bride.

"I am the vine, ye are the branches: He that abideth in me, and I in him, the same beareth much fruit: for apart from me ye can do nothing" (John 15:5 ASV).

Can you now see why Eve was called the "mother of all living"? She reveals what it means to be dark but lovely.

Chapter 4: The Dysfunction Revealed

n our brave attempts to please God, we have put our focus on the evidence of healing and revival being manifest through signs, wonders, and miracles. Don't misunderstand; I want to see the Word of God manifest in power and demonstration as much as any Christian. The Word declares this will occur, yet we have only seen waves of revival arise and then fall, leaving us in a whirlwind, wondering what happened and where did the move of God go? In the meantime, our families are still falling apart, with little knowledge of how to remedy the situation. We continue in begging God for answers to problems that are plaguing the church, while we as leaders have placed more and more requirements on the church so that God will respond to our obedience. Obedience to the law was not possible in the wilderness and is not possible in the way it is being portrayed now. "Obedience," according to our western mindset, leaves us in the wilderness attempting to accomplish what the children of God were never able to accomplish. This word *obedience* is actually a word that means "to hear me intimately."[7]

> A primitive root; to hear intelligently (often with implication of attention, obedience, etc.; causatively to tell, etc.): - X attentively, call (gather) together, X carefully, X certainly, consent, consider, be content, declare, X diligently, discern, give ear, (cause to, let, make to) hear (-ken, tell), X indeed, listen, make (a) noise, (be) obedient, obey, perceive, (make a) proclaim (-ation), publish, regard, report, shew (forth), (make a) sound, X surely, tell, understand, whosoever [heareth], witness.

God wanted relationship with man and to dwell in us intimately. That is still His desire today and shall ever be. "Hear, O Israel: The LORD our God is

---

7. Strongs H8085.

one LORD: And thou shalt love the LORD thy God with all thine heart, and with all thy soul, and with all thy might. And these words, which I command thee this day, shall be in thine heart" (Deuteronomy 6:4–6 KJV). In fact, God sent Moses three times to the children, seeking relationship, and they refused, telling Moses to go talk to God for them.

One of the greatest testaments against us as Christians is the dysfunction of the family and the lack of true love and peace in our homes. We have been decreeing and confessing the Word for forty-plus years yet with very little, if any, change. Where is this abundant life we are all seeking? We have tried many ways to fill our voids with no success. I propose we need to seek revival in the home, beginning in the marriage relationship. After all, that is where it started—with Adam and Eve.

Many have traded our possessions, self-worth, and even our voice in a fruitless effort to fill our emotional and sexual needs. This started when we lost our identity as a receiver and became judges. Many of us turned to food, alcohol, prescription drugs, work, children, religion, or anything else to acquire self-worth. This has only prolonged the issue and blinded us to the real problem. Men and women deal with this differently, and both seem hopeless. Women, attempting to justify our actions, often find fault in our husband or blame addictions for our demise. This kind of behavior may give way to depression, emotional numbness, and even physical illness in our bodies. Often, it will show up as a sick endocrine system. With good intent, husband, family, and friends suggest it may be hormonal and off we go to the doctor. Ultimately it results in a diagnosis and prescriptions, often with little—and short-lived—relief. This can cause one to sink further into more symptoms and more despair. For some it appears easier to just give up and choose to live alone, only to detest loneliness and find another man to start this madness all over again.

Every man I have worked with struggles with doing everything they have been taught and trying to fulfill their wives' requests. They try obeying the Bible and, like their leaders, attempt to give and do all that they can, only to feel like perpetual failures. They have become trapped in a prison of always hoping but never acquiring. I am talking about men of God who have served for forty-plus years as well as young men, handsome and financially sound. None of them feel like they have passion with their wives nor feel appreciated for what they have done or have attempted to do. Hopeless and rejected, they often withdraw into some form of addiction. If they are able to avoid an addiction, they resort to a passive escape into TV or some sport. If that fails, a divorce may be the only recourse. Unfortunately, they may find the same failure awaiting them in the next marriage.

I will use my own life experiences and the experiences of others to show the nature of the heart. These stories have accumulated over the past twenty-five-plus years. The pathway that I will present to you in this work is a result of seeking help for my spouse and me, as well as those who have come to us seeking help. I have worked with over a thousand men and women combined; all in some form of desperation, surviving with broken hearts. Often, it is their failing marriage that causes them to seek help.

We can only love others as we feel loved. The problem is, most don't. As a woman, I thought, *If men understood how to love their wives as Christ loved the Church and if that were actually happening, we would not have so many broken homes.*

While there is truth in that observation, women also need to know they are loved in order to be whole. If a woman is not already whole in her relationship with God, she will expect her husband to fill that void in her. This is an impossible task for any human. Only God can fill and heal a broken human soul. It is when the man and woman are whole and then share in each other's joy that others will take notice and want to experience what they are witnessing. The world is waiting to see this kind of love. Unfortunately, what they are seeing is not desirable. But how can a man love his wife in this way if he feels like a constant failure and his wife has set him up as her god? He is damned before he ever gets started. It is time for us to wake up and face the facts.

Since the age of nineteen, I have cried out to God, often on my face, looking for answers. I was told that a passionate marriage was just not possible and my idea of an abundant marriage was a joke. This was from Christian couples who had been married for years and in the church attempting to lead me. Why would I want to pattern my life after that? I refused. If God promised me abundance, then abundance was what I was going to have.

I have spent thirty years studying the heart, both physically and emotionally. I have learned when the heart feels a state of wholeness, it will spontaneously produce immediate and lasting change. The only obstacle that I have found that hinders the healing of the heart is our logic. If one refuses to lay down their intellect, they will not be able to enter into the heart-chambers of their own soul, much less the heart-chambers of others. It is in this part of us that our subconscious is forged or reformed in fear or love. The heart yearns to feel loved, and only God can fulfill that.

I propose that a global emotional revolution of heartfelt love and acceptance, first in the self and then in others, is on our horizon. I speak with boldness asking God to help me understand and speak the truth in love and transparency. I don't propose to know it all. But that which I do have, I now release unto you in this book. If you listen to my teachings on public media, you may hear me say, "In my current understanding." That is because I am ever learning, seeking for more and more truth. I am open for correction and God often obliges me with such. I trust that you will use your own discernment and prayerfully study this out for yourself to see if this work is in fact God-breathed and biblically sound.

Affection. What is it? Is it a necessity or a luxury? Is it physical or emotional? Could it be both? One without the other will leave the human spirit broken, thirsty, and longing for more than what physical affection alone can offer. Sex to some may appear to be only physical, and emotions are not required to experience sexual satisfaction. If that were true, then we could easily have a few steps or rules to follow, like a recipe to a chocolate cake, and there would be no sexual issues. To teach that we can take some steps or follow rules to experience lasting healthy sexual satisfaction has perpetuated and even exacerbated the breakdown of the marriage. The physical act of intercourse without the heart and emotional factor reduces sex to actions like unto dogs. God did not make us this way.

When a society treats sex as an emotionless action, it doesn't take long for the effects of such dishonor to become evident in every aspect of society. Our music, television shows, movies, clothes, business—all reflect such revelry. This may or may not seem like a personal preference and that one's sexuality isn't anyone's business; it sounds politically correct and acceptable until tragedy hits home with a daughter or wife; then one may conclude that lewd sex is an issue and one of great importance both privately and socially.

Sexuality without each partner first feeling whole in his and her own identity in God will not bring lasting fulfillment. It is the nature of God in us that makes us sexual beings in the first place, and trying to acquire wholeness outside of God in us is a futile illusion. The physical act of sex is the tangible expression of a much deeper eternal truth. Sex is the mirror image, not the eternal expression. When two hearts express their voices where both are honored and validated, that is unity.

Look at the word—*inter course*. Two voices entering into the same dwelling place in full unity and harmony. This is the mystery that sexual fulfillment reveals. Jesus is not desiring us as a physical bride to have physical intimacy. He desires to dwell in us, inside of our hearts, in unity and one voice expressing the fruit of love. This is the reason God gave us a body in the earth. He created us a physical body that God could make for Himself a dwelling that is tangible. The earth and the fullness is His and for His good pleasure. We are the object of that love and affection, emotionally.

Fundamentally when a woman receives emotional affection and feels cherished by her spouse, the physical union can bring a satisfaction beyond words. She cannot experience this until her broken heart has been made whole by her relationship with God. This keeps her from placing the responsibility of her emotional wellness onto her spouse. Only after I had exhausted every measure to find wholeness in my union with my earthly spouse and failed was I compelled to seek out God for answers. My marriage was the perfect union to reveal to me in my heart what I was really searching for. I was searching for love, and God is love. The problem is, I had cut off my heart for fear of rejection. I had built a wall around my spiritual female heart, my "Eve Part."

"Let the husband render to his wife the affection due her, and likewise also the wife to her husband" (1 Corinthians 7:3 NKJV). I have heard ministers use this Scripture to give a woman marital advice. It is common practice to advise that she never withhold sexual relations from her spouse except for prayer and fasting. I have even heard leaders say that if a woman did withhold sex from her husband and he commits adultery, it would be her fault. What! I am appalled at such ignorance. Can a father with a clear conscience advise his daughter to agree to such a disgrace? This attitude places the wife with little more value than a prostitute. This lack of understanding the woman's heart and its part in her sexuality has caused many women to fornicate with their own husbands.

No Longer Dis-Eve'd

This type of sex will leave her feeling dirty and can kill her affection for her husband altogether. If a woman continues to offer her husband sex as a duty or a commitment, she will grow numb toward him and eventually the relationship will die. Some couples actually continue to live together as partners without passion while others will find their escape by way of divorce or extra-marital affairs.

Humans enter this world with a need to be nurtured and cared for physically and emotionally. As we mature, we develop a desire for sexual affection. This does not mean our need for emotional affection disappears. On the contrary, our emotional affections are necessary in order for us to experience lasting sexual satisfaction with our spouse.

Moreover, when women feel connected through emotional affirmation, the sex drive is healthy and often times greater than a man's. Unfortunately, most women don't understand their own heart, and if they cannot understand their own heart, how can they expect their husband to? In addition, most men are less capable of understanding their emotions and are in need of help from the women. In scientific studies, little boys are innately less capable of expressing their emotions than little girls. Women who are fashioned from and represent the inside are naturally emotional. In fact, they have a drive to be emotionally satisfied that is as powerful as their sex drive. It is so strong that it can actually enhance or kill their libido.

Moreover, generation after generation we have taught our children to avoid emotional pain and to control our feelings. In addition, we have been taught that feelings are not trustworthy, setting us up for emotional stress with no remedy. It is time to face our unhealthy emotional condition and heal. This may be the reason so many men feel inferior emotionally. No wonder so many couples are hopeless.

Without emotional guidance, women have grown weary, withdrawn, and discontent, leaving their husbands feeling like failures. The good news is, wholeness in the emotions—first with God, then with ourselves—presents a healthy pathway for our husbands. The result is so satisfying for both the male and female, men are actually asking Michael and me to teach them more about the emotions and how to nurture them. We had two couples over the age of seventy proclaim:

"Where were ya'll twenty-five years ago? We have never experienced lovemaking like that. Every couple needs to have their hearts healed."

We agree, and that is why we are sharing our story.

As I lay out the pathway through Scripture, I will attempt to bring it all together in a practical manner so that you can actually experience what I am talking about. Remember, spiritual things cannot be seen with the eyes in our heads, so I will be showing you how to observe with the eyes of the heart what the eyes of our logic cannot see. In order to explain emotional intimacy, we must compare the seen to the unseen.

Note the Scriptures gave instruction to the man first and then to the woman. Such wisdom portrayed in the Scriptures reveals the woman's sexuality is in the heart and is her fundamental sexual need. Without emotional fulfillment, sex can actually feel dirty and appalling. Sex without emotional fulfillment can and often does bring about a measure of satisfaction; however, it will wane quickly, giving way to routine and apathy. It is common for the wife to keep these feelings hidden so that she doesn't wound her husband. Though the intention may be honorable, this type of dishonor can lend to divorce, affairs, multiple marriages, or partners fostering a society with no honor for the marriage union.

A woman's body is created to work physically in harmony with her heart. When a woman's heart is tender and functioning properly, she has a built-in safety mechanism to promote chastity and faithfulness with passion toward her lover. Her body is made to feel wonderful and free with the man who holds her heart and, therefore, her body. Moreover, if a man who does not hold her heart, attempts to approach her in any sexual or inappropriate way, it will cause her skin to crawl. This is to keep her from being a sex object. Her skin should crawl if anyone touches her body sexually but does not hold her heart and cherish it. Her husband is not exempt from this natural response. If he dishonors her heart, she will shut down emotionally as God created her to. She is made this way. Sex is an emotional, heartfelt physical expression of two hearts that are already one emotionally.

Sex is not the pathway to intimacy. Emotional intimacy is the pathway to amazing, passionate sex.

No Longer Dis-Eve'd

Men, take note here and now. When a woman is free in your arms emotionally, she can reach places in physical intimacy that are beyond comprehension. A woman's ability to reach climax is not based on the man's actions alone; it is based predominantly on how her heart feels. If a woman refuses to listen to her heart and continues to have sex when the heart is broken, withdrawn, and screaming "No!" her heart will disconnect from her womb. Numbness will become her natural state. When a woman ignores her heart and disconnect occurs, she will often use sex to try to feel whole again. If a woman was abused sexually or if she did not value herself as a woman, the disconnect will take place very early in childhood. If this happens, her heart will feel separated and often hopeless in lovemaking. At this point, the very thing that was designed to protect her has now become the reason for her sexual dysfunction or her allowing her own body to be dishonored sexually.

Abused children are not allowed to listen to their hearts. This causes the little heart to disconnect in order to protect the heart while the body is being violated. The heart is designed to wait patiently until we are ready to go back into our pain and heal. I have worked with countless women and helped the inner child's heart to heal and reconnect. The result was a miracle in that she was finally able to experience healthy, passionate lovemaking with her spouse.

Once a woman's heart waxes cold, she will have an unnatural affection and may easily resort to sex trying to feel whole. This will not work and actually will make her feel less loved. Inside of the marriage, her feelings of love and affection toward her husband often cry out for healing as she seeks to experience true sexual intimacy with her spouse. Sadly, her spouse often blames himself, and this blame perpetuates his feelings of failure. When a man is afforded this truth, the love for his wife will impel him to protect her heart as though it was his own body as stated in the Bible: "Even so ought husbands also to love their own wives as their own bodies. He that loveth his own wife loveth himself: for no man ever hated his own flesh; but nourisheth and cherisheth it, even as Christ also the church" (Ephesians 5:28-29 ASV).

Most women have felt feelings of disgust with the men they love but have kept silent about such feelings. This is living a lie, and we as women are contributing to the demise of our relationships if we keep such feelings secret. Men need to know the truth of our hearts, and they can be trusted with this truth when presented in a safe environment. My husband and I often work with couples to help uncover these hidden sorrows. The good news is we can heal, and most can heal quite rapidly.

When I first began to ask women in front of their spouse if they ever felt dirty after having sex with their spouse, they were afraid to tell the truth. This is a form of betrayal. When the men heard this truth, they would become sad and angry. It would cause them to question why and really listen to the hearts of the women they loved. It is sad to see wonderful men who have spent years doing everything they knew to please their wives only to find out that the one they love has often hid her pain and endured their lovemaking as if it were a duty. It is just as painful to discover that she has been having sex out of pity to avoid hurting him.

After the anger is felt, and with assistance, the man can go deep into his heart and the heart of his wife. It is here their tears begin to flow and healing begins. Suffering together produces an amazing bond of healing. It is this kind of truth that opens the pathway for true healing and hope. Men often realize that this is a good thing that she is created in this fashion. They can see how if they will cherish the heart and feelings of their wives their relationships will heal and become full of passion and joy. This kind of loving relationship is stronger than the grave, whereas commitment and duty die in our courts every day.

I am not suggesting that a woman should give her husband the cold shoulder, nor should she use sex as a means of manipulation to make her feel loved and whole. Moreover, I am not excusing extra-marital affairs for the man or the woman. I am simply explaining what I have witnessed to be true in many Christian marriages. If a man does not understand how the heart-womb connection works, it is easy to assume that the woman is manipulating him. This false conclusion aids in avoiding the real issue of intimacy and leads to looking for outside remedies. I have witnessed this quite a bit in the church as men and women are given list of things expected in the roles they hold as man and wife.

This can and often does lead to another form of control and manipulation rather than spontaneous relationship born out of intimacy.

When love rules, there are no rules needed. Using sex or rules to control a relationship is by no means acceptable. Marriage out of duty or obligation is not abundant or full of joy. Trading actions for sex is a form of prostitution and will kill the relationship. God did not mess up when he made us as opposites. On the contrary, our very natures are perfect to bring us into relationship with God and each other.

To tell a woman that she must have sex because she is married reduces the relationship down to a law, a contract. The law kills; that is the very nature of the law. Spirit, on the other hand, brings life. Law equals rules, and spirit is spontaneous feelings from the heart. Once the emotional relationship dies, infidelity will often be the result. What a tragedy. Many wonderful people who really loved each other have found themselves in such a situation with no one to help or to warn them of these pitfalls.

Exposing these dangers, digging deep into our broken hearts, and allowing God to heal them is the biblical pathway for healthy sexual intimacy. This is the beginning of our transformation. Truth plus nothing is what sets us free. Fear of feeling pain has held us prisoner for way too long. It is never too late to wake up and face our intimacy issues.

Boundaries are another form of control that is often used beyond what is healthy. Let me be clear on this topic. When a person is wounded and coming out of codependency or control, boundaries can be a very healthy means to heal. However, once the heart is whole, boundaries could become another set of rules that can and often do take the place of relationship with God. Like a cast on a broken foot, I want it removed after the bone has healed. If the cast (boundaries) is not removed, the entire body suffers.

Women usually find it is easier to face emotional and sexual issues openly and candidly. When they do, they pave the way for men to understand what a woman needs in relationship. I warn women who take this path that one of two things will happen with their spouse. They will usually get mad at first but then want the same kind of help, ending in a restored passionate marriage. Or, they will refuse true emotional intimacy and leave. Most couples heal quite quickly, but some refuse to leave logic and abandon the heart, resulting in divorce.

A woman keeping silent about her sexual disconnect has caused many a good man to lose his wife to a would-be player who knows how to say all the right emotional words with no true meaning behind them. This tragedy needs to stop. Humans are born with an emotional and sexual appetite. Our lack of understanding in these areas has left the fabric of the family unit in ruins.

The new laws defining marriage, global gender confusion, political correctness, rampant divorce, domestic violence, and sexual abuse are results of our ignorance. Ephesians tells us that marriage between a man and a woman is the very thing in this earth that reveals the mystery of Christ and His bride. The Kingdom of God has suffered violence, and it is time that the violent take it back by force. The violence that I am speaking of is the violence against the kingdom that is in our hearts—the emotions, our Eve part. All humans, men and women, have an "Eve" part inside.

Jesus Himself said the kingdom is inside of us. This is a kingdom where love rules. "He that loveth not knoweth not God; for God is love" (1 John 4:8 KJV) Love is a person, not an action. Love is experienced in the feelings. It is the ears and eyes of the heart that are able to see and hear love.

Science has revealed that emotions are the only thing known to man that transcend space and time. Scripture confirms this science when it tells us that love is stronger than the grave and is eternal. Feelings of rejection have moved some to murder and others to suicide, while feeling loved has caused people to lay down their lives even for a stranger. Love is a force that must be reckoned with. It is time for us to understand this kingdom that is in our hearts and take it back. Ecclesiastes tells us that inside the heart lies eternity.

It is the actual heart through which God Himself said He would lead us by. God is love, and when we feel the presence of love we are moved by love not fear. Our culture, however, has attempted to teach us to resist emotions or control them by only allowing positive emotions into our hearts. This is an illusion that has caused our hearts to be calloused, producing spiritual blindness and deafness, because it is through pain that the heart is awakened. True freedom is to no longer need to resist any of our emotions. Rather, we are to lift them up to God and admit to our inability to rightly divide truth without God's divine direction. It is in seeking the heart that we acquire the mind of the Holy Spirit. In the fourth chapter of Ephesians, we are told to put away bitterness, wrath, anger, clamor, and evil speaking. This phrase *put away* comes from the Greek word *epairo*, which means to raise up. It derived from the Hebrew word *nasa*, which means to lift up, take up, and to raise the voice as in to cry out for help, and at the same time keep the mind in suspense while waiting for God to deliver. In so doing, we can face all truth and have deep spiritual intimacy with God and healthy appropriate intimacy with our spouses, our children, and others.

So what does it mean "be put away from you"? It means to lift up bitterness, wrath, anger, clamour, and evil speaking and separate it in order to complete or be at rest. This is the process of maturing and being perfected through suffering. Moreover, in Ephesians 4:19 being past our feelings comes from the word *apalgeo*, which is to become apathetic separating from it as a form of completion which is to surrender unto lasciviousness which is filthy wantonness or vanity (Strong's G524). It goes on to say that Christ did not teach us this. In fact, He came to suffer with us and to show us the way to suffer unto completion. The act of trying to do away with these painful emotions and avoiding them will produce a life of coping with lasciviousness, uncleanness, and greediness. However, if we lift up all of our painful suffering emotions unto God and allow God to use them to perfect us and mature our limbic brain, we then have our senses exercised and are able to go into deeper relationship with God as our nature shifts from the fight or flight mode into counting all suffering as a joy and honor to be counted worthy to suffer with Him. In addition, our hearts are purified as this pain like fire and the love of God dwelling in us causes us to trust all things, hope all things, believe all things, and not keep any record of wrong that has been done to us. This is the fruit of not running from any emotion but rather lifting them all up to God as a gift of fire and the pathway of healing for our broken hearts. This is the nature of our living soul. It hungers and needs to be filled.

Woman came from the inside of the male, next to his heart. Scripture actually tells us that God put the man in a trance (just a side note, it never said He woke him up) and took his rib and formed the woman. Her nature existed prior to being given her form in the flesh. They were two in one. She started out as part of him, but on the inside of him, unable to be experienced. Their unborn, unseen children were already in their loins, yet they too were hidden in his seed and her ovum. Here is the pattern of the father, mother, and child.

"For the invisible things of him from the creation of the world are clearly seen, being understood by the things that are made, even his eternal power and Godhead; so that they are without excuse" (Romans 1:20 KJV). It is revealed in the basics of all creation. Let us start by looking at the atom/Adam as a positive, negative, and a neutral; a man is the positive giver, a woman is the negative receiver, and their children remain neutral where all things are possible when the two (+-) become one. Then came the commission to be fruitful and multiply. Their nature of oneness would compel them into a union of sexual intercourse. This cycle of union and separation is the mystery of life in God through Christ, our husband. Moreover, we will see throughout this book that without both the giver and the receiver, that which is concealed or hidden could not be revealed. Therefore, when we deny our Eve/receiver nature we surrender the "all things are possible" manifesting in and through us as the bride. It is in and though the place where our emotions live that the power of love can be deposited by God and then shine out of us manifesting as the fruit of the Spirit of God—love, joy, peace, patience, kindness, goodness, faithfulness, gentleness, and self-control. The power of God and the Godhead are all revealed in these three in all things created—positive, negative, and neutral. The female nature reveals the negative glory, energy, power that must be embraced in order for the fullness of God's Word to be birthed. This is the mystery of the marriage of Christ and His bride that is revealed in the human marriage union.

The woman is still longing to live in the heart of her husband where emotional union fills her with passions that buckle her knees and take her breath away. A passion that she would rather die than live without. The problem is, this kind of passion cannot exist within a dead, numb, calloused, broken, and medicated heart. The heart must be resurrected and be willing to feel all emotions—both the negative and the positive. Killing joy is easy, but killing pain is not possible. In our ignorant attempts to numb our sorrows, we have waxed cold and built fake walls of protection. Let's look at our true desires and find our way back to truth and life.

What are "the deep desires of a woman's heart"? A special, soft touch by his strong hand; that deep look into her eyes that says something words cannot say; someone who likes her just the way she is; someone with whom she will feel alive, interesting, and fun to be with; someone who cares about her needs, likes, desires, and thoughts; a man who will look at her when she has something to say, even if it is not really that important; the look that says, *You are important and I care what you think and how you feel.*

Calm down, fellas. This is not a chore for the man whose heart is full of emotions and who is living to his fullest, true self. Most men, unknowingly, have long ago taken off their true identity in an effort to survive or find acceptance. Often a man will say, "That is just who I am and I am not changing." The truth is, when men are young boys they often suffer being bullied, controlled, manipulated—ultimately finding themselves forged into some image other than who God created them to be. As a means of survival, the young boy had to change to self-protect. It is time men get real and find their true self, not the one they were "forced" to become. When men heal, they often are pleasantly surprised at how amazing they really are. No longer are they bound by anger and fear of failure.

The way a man looks at his wife's body and into her eyes; his voice and the tone of it when he speaks to her; the feel of his hand in hers, strong yet gentle; how he touches her shoulder only if and when the chemistry permits; beyond the shoulder and to the waist, if and only if her heart is cherished can this touch be accepted and invited freely. Face to face, as the hearts have become one and then, as a result, find themselves in an intimate kiss. This progression leads on into a deeper trust where he is invited to touch the body fully without restraint. Then moving forward, physical intimacy is expressed as a freedom that has already been consummated in the heart, which gives reign to proceed to the torso and touching below the waist and on to full intercourse. Moving too fast and without regard to the conditions of the heart can and will provoke unwanted division. The heart condition is what causes the woman to yield her body without restraint and in full passion.

Because men are mostly physical, they may attempt to proceed not realizing that the woman's heart is not open and willing. If a women's heart is saying no but she has blocked it out because of any fear, she may allow the man to proceed without understanding and separations can persist undetected. Verbal communication from the woman is paramount. However, if the woman is not healed emotionally, she will not speak up, to both their detriment. Verbal skills to discuss these matters in a healthy and effective manner must be developed. Now is the time for change. We are bone of his bone and flesh of his flesh.

Let us return to Adam's original response when he saw Eve; "And Adam said, This is now bone of my bones, and flesh of my flesh: she shall be called Woman, because she was taken out of Man" (Genesis 2:23 KJV; emphasis mine). It is time for us to B-One!

Chapter 5: A Woman's Feelings on Trial

All good gifts come from God, including the gifts we receive through each other. If we think it is another person's duty to meet all the physical needs but the heart is not whole in God first, trying to meet these needs will become a chore. We must understand the human body and accept the foundational truth that abundant life flows first from God through the heart. When we are whole and feel loved by God in our hearts, then we honor God, ourselves, and others. Moreover, we will spontaneously require others to honor us. If another attempts to dishonor us, our hearts will speak to us in pain. This pain is like a check engine light on the dashboard of our automobile. The pain is our pathway to healing the subconscious, which brings about healed feelings of wholeness in God. Avoiding the pain will cause us to miss the mark, the calculation, the wonder, therefore our miracle. If we ignore our check engine light and our oil runs dry, we can burn up our engine. Likewise, if we ignore or mitigate our pain, we will miss the warning sign and dishonor our own hearts. We set the standard by which all others will honor or dishonor us.

A woman's basic need is to feel loved and secure emotionally. These feelings can be experienced when we are spiritually connected, heard, and treated with equality. Moreover, we desire a nurturing relationship to keep us feeling loved. After Adam and Eve ate from the tree of the knowledge of good and evil, God said the woman would desire her husband and that he would rule over her. Women have put men in the place of God and expect their husbands to accomplish and fulfill their basic needs.

God will use the husband to gift the wife with many wonderful gifts, but all good gifts come from God and not man. Humans are designed to get their deep needs met by God. It all started in the Garden of Eden, and like Eve we eat from our logical knowledge and still look to our Adam to fulfill us.

No Longer Dis-Eve'd

We as women have believed that our lover is the one through whom we will experience wholeness. Often at first, the man will seem to provoke this sense of unity. When we feel this unity in the relationship, we will desire to move forward to the point where trust is established and then, as a woman, we will desire to be touched intimately, yet not in a sexual way.

In addition, women will want to feel protected. As the weaker vessel, if she feels safe, she will want to advance the relationship.

However, moving too fast in a physical way can undermine her need to feel protected. Respect is another requirement and must remain a vital part of the relationship both ways. This natural progression will provoke the desire in her for intimacy with touch and gentleness.

These are touches like hand to face, hand to hair, and gentle kisses that are deeply affectionate yet not sexual in nature. These are not steps nor should they be portrayed as steps. They often occur naturally when a woman's heart is intact, healthy, and alive. If a woman is numb, she will skip many if not all and go right to sex in an attempt to feel satisfaction, only to find more discontentment.

Most women report that at the beginning of their relationship with their spouse, this natural progression existed, but over time waxed cold. The men report no awareness that any of these stages existed. He has no conscious knowledge of the gentle progression. It appears to be an instinctive response by the man, as the woman allows him to move in closer and closer, with the man's objective being sexual intercourse.

In this manner, the woman assumes that he is aware, and she is in a state of euphoria that he is so attentive. As things progress to sexual contact and then intercourse, the man appears to feel a sense of accomplishment and no longer continues in the original progression of intimacy. Once intercourse has occurred, the man may feel that her body is accessible to him at all times. He may assume that she feels and responds in the same fashion as his male body. If the natural progression is abandoned, the woman will feel like an object and possibly begin to reject the man's advances. In his wounded and unsure state, he may revert unknowingly back to the natural progression with success. He feels restored and she feels hopeful that he understood and will not repeat the behavior of treating her body like an object.

The problem with this is that neither of them have the communication skills nor the awareness that their perceptions are different. In time, this yo-yo effect can become a point of contention and may actually be sabotaging the relationship.

Moreover, women often desire gentleness and cuddling after lovemaking yet don't understand that men are physically not built to provide such a request. The man after making love has a chemical released into the bloodstream that is actually a natural sedative. It is necessary for the man to restore his testosterone that was just depleted.

Women need to reminisce to allow their sexual passions to dissipate. Due to the euphoria and chemical state of her body, she needs this time to allow her hormones to subside. This is because a woman can experience multiple climaxes and much longer orgasms than men. Therefore, her body will remain ready after an initial orgasm, as it may not be the only one. If a woman doesn't understand the physiological reasons for these differences, she may put an expectation on her lover that he is not able to keep. It is okay for the man to sleep and the woman to stay awake and reminisce with gratitude and bliss. I can hear the men saying, "Yes, for God's sake let me sleep, woman."

Years ago, I read that in the football game of life, men have one goal in mind: "touchdown." Women, however, want to enjoy every yard line and stop to look at the wild flowers growing on the field. Another analogy that I heard was men are like a gas stove; turn them on and they are hot; turn them off and they are off. Women, on the other hand, are like an electric stove top; it takes time to heat up and time to cool down.

Women love to say, "Yeah, that's right, he needs to give me time to warm up." Well, it cuts both ways, ladies. When it comes to the emotions, men need to warm up, and they need to understand emotions before they can just go there.

As little boys, they have been taught not to cry and that emotions show lack of strength. Moreover, women are described as emotional and that could threaten his manhood if he doesn't understand what we as women are asking for and needing from them. I have met very few women who are able to express their own emotions, yet blame their poor relationship on the fact that their spouse does not know their heart. As true as that may be, we too as women need to first learn our own hearts and allow God to heal them.

No Longer Dis-Eve'd

Then we will not be codependent on another person in order to feel secure and loved. On the contrary, we will feel loved, whole, and complete in God, and thereby able to share our hearts and bodies in a healthy manner with our husband.

It remains a mystery to me that men instinctively connect with our emotions when they are in the hunting mode and are trying to win our hearts. However, after that has been accomplished and they have the woman's hand in marriage or her body in bed, something happens and they get a severe attack of emotional amnesia.

Suddenly, a man not only can't remember what a woman's emotions are or how to treat them, he cannot comprehend what he did before marriage that made her feel so loved and understood. The hunt is over, and as women we can be left feeling like an animal trophy on the wall for show rather than an intimate woman in love with the man she married.

In my attempt to help my husband understand this dilemma, I asked him:

"Do you put on your hunting clothes, your boots, deer scent, and load your gun, then bring it into the living room before showing someone your trophy deer on the wall? Obviously not! Well, do I look like a stuffed trophy on the wall to you? So, you say the hunt is over, yet I am not dead, and neither am I on the wall. What it took to get me is what it will take to keep me."

We discussed how in our dating stage, for some reason unbeknownst to him or me, he cherished my heart, looked into my eyes, and listened to my feelings. He was blind to my faults and said all the right things spontaneously. He wanted to spend every moment that he had free with me and even gave up time for himself and sacrificed what he liked just to come visit and hold my hand. He gave me soft yet respectful, appropriate touches.

He bragged on me to others—in front of me. It was like a dream. Well, it must have been, because when I walked down the aisle and said "I do," we woke up.

At this time, I was looking to him to meet my needs, not God. In my illusion, I not only expected him to, and he did, I was taught that it was his duty as my husband. I expected my emotional wellness to come from him.

I got in the car on the way to the wedding reception and thought, What happened? Who is this guy? And what did you do with my husband? Where is the guy I fell in love with? Because he is the one whom I gave my heart to, and I am not sure I know who you are. Without cause or explanation, Michael shifted from the boyfriend who was wooing my heart to the husband who now had the job of protecting me and providing for me. Without any self-awareness, he had become my god. It took us years to discover what had taken place inside of him. Moreover, many men and women we have counseled over the years confess they experienced the same shift.

Soon after our wedding night, I devised a plan to get him back.

Very quickly, all I could see were his faults. He became this guy who expected me to cook and clean like his mother, meet his every need on his time frame, treat me like his daughter by expecting me to obey and conform to all of his requests without question; and oh, by the way, after the game and before going to sleep, have a blissful time of lovemaking! What? Treating me like a daughter and then expecting to make love? Yuck! Girls don't make love to their daddies. Submission cuts both ways, I thought.

I would work all day, come home, cook, clean, serve, wash clothes, balance the checkbook, and be physical with this guy who was now my husband, and all with no affection toward my heart. Doesn't it say somewhere in the Bible for husbands to likewise give the affections due his wife?

He didn't understand me. He felt overwhelmed with a sense of expectations that he had no idea how to fill. How could he fulfill expectations that he didn't understand and I could not explain? Expectations that I had in my heart and mind, that truly only God could fulfill.

In his mind, the act of making love was being emotional. Most men communicate in steps and rules. Sports, war, work, and tasks are normal and easy to learn. However, in the arena of emotions, there are no rules and they are infinite. They have no hash tags, or buttons, or steps. Society has taught men their entire life that to feel would only cause them problems. I was now asking my husband to be emotional with no real understanding of my request. At this point in our lives we were both at a loss, feeling handicapped with no one to turn to.

Everywhere I read, listened, or searched, I was told you can't trust your emotions. Here are some of the most common myths we are told about our emotions:

- **Feelings don't always tell the truth.**
- **How you feel is not how you are.**
- **Maturity is valuing your feelings without letting them determine your decisions.**
- **If you change your mind your feelings will follow.**
- **True love is an act of your will, not an emotion you feel.**

Well, let me tell you, it only takes a "part" truth to convince us that something is accurate. All of this sounds good, but the results are slavery and misery.

Remember the two parts of the brain where our memories are located? The place where memories are connected directly to our emotions is in the limbic brain, and the data storage memory is in the frontal lobe.

The amygdala is in the limbic brain. It houses our memories that are formed with and by the emotions, weaving together the facts of an experience, the feelings that resulted, and the chemical recordings of the five senses. Together they calculate a conclusion and store its calculation to assist the body as an instinctual, spontaneous survival mechanism.

The frontal lobe is the place where our data is stored and is not formed with our emotions. Our rational frontal lobe can affect our limbic somewhat, and therefore can help to calm down our emotions through self-talk. This reaction to our emotional state actually makes the logical brain seem reliable and safe. The frontal lobe is task-oriented as well as a reward-seeking calculator. It will actually work against the emotions in an attempt to experience relief of pain. Relief is the reward that the logical brain was seeking. It can bring temporary relief, but it cannot permanently change our feelings. Moreover, it cannot fix any lie that is held as truth in the amygdala. Because feelings create the emotional memories and calculate facts through our feelings, no amount of logic can erase the calculated emotional belief. These emotional threads can only be transformed by the same emotions that formed them. It is kind of like a locked door. The only key that can open the door is the same one that locked it. So if rejection locked it, then rejection is needed to open it, so that acceptance can be deposited into that memory.

Remember all of the forty-thousand neurites that make up the heart-brain? This part of the heart is connected to the amygdala. Only by healing the emotions can the subconscious heal and feel loved. Knowing this truth allows us to look at five myths about emotions. By understanding the facts about how emotions work, we can have an understanding that yields lasting success, freedom, and spontaneous intimacy.

Let's look at each of them and apply what we have learned about the brain and its relationship with the heart.

1) We have been told that our feelings don't always tell the truth. The truth is, even though I am loved by God, I can sometimes feel rejected. Therefore, my feelings were telling me the truth. Without this pain, I would not realize that I was believing the lie in my amygdala, because in my logical brain I believed I was loved. This pain is the pathway to remove the lie from my emotional memory. It must be corrected in my amygdala or I will remain double-minded. Therefore, my feelings were for me to lead me into the whole truth. If I only use my knowledge to tell myself that I am loved, then I stay stuck in the lie and I will wrestle with rejection over and over yet never overcome the fear of rejection. So how can I remedy this?

I must take note of the original feeling that is being presented, go into that feeling and ask God to show me how that lie was embedded into my amygdala, then ask God to change that part of my brain. Now my feelings will match the truth that God revealed and not the facts of my past to find my identity.

2) We have been told the way we feel is not how we truly are. The truth is, as a man thinks, so is he, and whatever we believe we shall have. I had been instructed to just change my thinking and confess positive affirmations over my situation. Feelings that are based in my past experiences are held in my memory in the amygdala and will produce in my life what it holds to be true.

This happens even if my perception was distorted by my past experiences and I am believing a lie. The memories are electronic and magnetic. Together they proceed out of my body and into the bio-magnetic field as seeds. The emotional beliefs are the blueprints of our reality. Only changing the logical thought and not addressing the source in the amygdala will cause me to wrestle again and again with the same old lie held in the emotional memory. Each re-occurrence is the grace afforded us to renew our emotional memories.

This must shift from the old lie, which is filled with some facts. Change can only occur through the same pain that holds the lie in that part of the memory.

No Longer Dis-Eve'd

Our brains take a T-minus-1 snapshot of our painful experiences in an effort to survive. It is a beast or animal instinct. It will release into our bloodstream cortisol and adrenalin to give us the necessary energy to fight or run. The only way to change this T-1 memory is to go back into the memory and add new emotions filled with love, compassion, care, and gratitude. When the old neurite expands as a result of the painful memory, new information can be deposited chemically. This actually heals the emotional memory completely. I have seen this over and over, and it is actually teachable and duplicable. Every person I have used this technique with has healed in literally as little as three minutes.

Scripture calls this *in the twinkling of an eye*. This affects my entire life, because it changes my beliefs and thoughts. I shall have whatever I believe or hold to be true. So here again the emotions are to reveal where the lies are so that I can know who I really am, not what my past tells me that I am.

3) We have been told that to value our feelings without letting them determine our decisions is maturity. The truth is, to truly value feelings with maturity means to use our feelings that are inside of our hearts to reveal the places in our heart-brain and limbic brain that are stuck in past perceptions. Then have the courage to allow the feelings to transform the old perception, held in the limbic that holds the lies, to be transformed with truth. In so doing, the heart-brain connection will hold fast to the truth of our identity in God, rather than our identity of who others, or our experiences, have told us we are. To trust in a past or learned experience is found in the Hebrew word *nachash* ("naw-khawsh," Strong's H5175). In the English translation, it is the word *serpent*. "Now the serpent was more subtle than any beast of the field which Jehovah God had made" (Genesis 3:1 ASV). In addition to learned experiences, it means "to hiss, to whisper, to spell (as in a word), to divine, to learn by experiences, to diligently observe." To realize that trusting in my learned experiences is the same as yielding to the serpent blew my mind. However, this revelation of the brain has shown me how and why we get stuck in our self-sabotaging cycles of trusting in our primitive limbic calculation to self-defend or hide. This is what the knowledge of good and evil produces—wilderness cycles just like the children of God in the desert after leaving Egypt.

78

Our learned experiences are recorded in both the logical and emotional brains. They actually calculate all the time. Because our logical brain is weaker than our emotional brain, both electronically and magnetically, we are damned to respond to our old broken emotions and run like a beast or fight like a beast. It is the calculation of the beast nature in us. Until our emotions are healed, we will live out of this calculation. Just a side note: the word *calculation* is the same word as "mark." Therefore, we could call this the calculation or "mark of the beast."

4) We have been told if we change our minds our feelings will follow. The truth is, the only true change takes place where the heart and the mind come together and are in unity. This only takes place in the heart-brain and limbic brain, *not* the frontal lobe. So, we can add all the knowledge of the entire universe to our frontal lobe and if the truth does not enter the heart through the heart-brain connection, then we are just acquiring knowledge in our frontal lobe and not truth in our heart-brain. Knowledge alone will only puff us up. Remember the heart magnetism? It is 5,000 times stronger than the frontal lobe. Moreover, the heart's electric frequency is 100 times stronger than the frontal lobe. Therefore, it is scientifically impossible to override the heart with logic. To trust in our own understanding is what the Bible tells us *not* to do. This is like trusting the merry-go-round in our head to override the Clydesdale horses in our hearts. Going around and around in the same cycles for years provoked me to anger. It was this anger that opened my eyes and caused me to seek answers beyond traditional teachings.

5) We have been told true love is an act of our will, not an emotion that we feel. The truth is, love is a person who can be felt in our emotions. God is an eternal being and God is love. Every human relationship is birthed in emotions and will live or die there. It is with the emotions that the power of love is experienced in the human heart. If it were possible for us to just choose to do good and then do it, there would be no divorce, gluttony, drunkenness, depression, sickness, disease, etc.

Love is of the spirit and against such there is no law or rule. I know many who have done things because it is the right thing to do. The Word says that if I can know and reveal all truth, even all mysteries, speak in all languages—even the languages of the angels—and if I give my body to be burned, yet have not love (God, experienced in the heart through the feelings of love and compassion), then I am just a loud noise. Think about it. If a man and woman make love just because they are married but they do not experience the feelings of love, that would be called sex, not lovemaking. That is what dogs do. I am not willing to settle for that kind of relationship, are you?

However, I do not want love out of commitment nor duty. I want a heartfelt relationship established in God who is love and that is stronger than death.

What is your desire? If controlling your emotions and living out of rules is working for you, then I am happy for you. I encourage you to keep controlling them. However, if you have tried this life, like I did, and found that it was not full of righteousness, peace, and joy—if your life is not abundant and full—then I suggest that you give up your commitment to love. I suggest that you fall into the arms of the one who is Love, Jesus, and be one with Love (Jesus) and let Love flow through you. Where Love rules there is no need for rules. Loving actions are spontaneous results of our relationship with God. Love is not a life of choosing to do good; it is a life of passion with the source of passion. I often tell others: You keep your rules and I shall cry out to my God, "Give me passion or give me death." Either we can have life abundant, or the Word is a lie. I am fully persuaded that the Word, Jesus, is Truth and He cannot lie nor break His promises.

I read in the Bible that a wise man studies what to say. So, I began my search to find a new vocabulary that could reach into people's hearts and explain what was in mine. If I was going to have this life that I was promised and it was inside of me, then I was going to have to search deep inside my heart and learn to live from that perspective. It was time to stop going to people who did not have this life I desired. I realized that what I was doing was kind of like going to the homeless to learn how to be a millionaire.

In the meantime, while I was on this relentless search to see what was in my heart and how it worked, we continued as husband and wife—going to church, reading our Bible, tithing, doing good, taking classes, going to Sunday school, following all the rules. We learned our love language and learned how to pray one hour every day. We tried these steps and rules only to find more and more failure.

Michael worked hard, did his chores, raised a garden, and tried to follow the rules that accompanied the traditional holidays. I worked hard, was a stay-at-home mom, was a great cook, kept the house, canned the garden veggies, visited his mom and mine. I dressed appropriately to keep myself attractive and met him at the door. I made sure the food was ready on the table, the house was spotless, and the children were well-behaved. We all would greet Michael at the door and sit as a family for dinner. We were the model family, and even our pastors and leaders agreed. Sometimes we were even commended openly, as it was fitting to give honor where honor was due. Looking back, this makes me nauseous.

What was happening? How could this love we shared go so wrong? We were committed, faithful, consistent, and we loved each other. We both loved God. Michael felt like everything was good. The kids were happy, our bills were paid, and we were keeping all the rules. He did not understand how I was so discontent. As a woman, I tried everything to no avail. *It must be me,* I thought. I was so tired of being the one who needed to change. It had been only my responsibility since we married. This was now going on seven years and I was tired.

In my desperation, I cried out, "God, please show me what to do. Open his eyes and show him. Help! Please help!"

Chapter 6: God's Response

M y child, you are not his Holy Spirit, I am." Ouch! That hurt. If you are suffering as we were, I have a few things that I learned that may help you too. I do not claim that what worked for me will answer all of your problems, but I know that God's principles are truth and life. Gravity works for those who believe in God and for those who do not. So, if you are not so sure about your belief in God, just let my story help you, and maybe you will find the love that is God.

I was married in 1985 to my best friend. He was kind, loving and compassionate. He would help the stranger and give the shirt off of his back. He was trustworthy and filled with integrity. He loved me before I could love myself. I had been molested by my prior boyfriend, and I felt dirty and unlovable. On our second date, he told me that he loved me. I told him that I was not having sex with him, and if he was saying that just so he could get me to have sex with him he could just take that lie somewhere else.

He looked me straight in the eyes and he said, "I do love you and I will say it whenever I feel like it; and you can receive it or not, but I will say it. I love you."

My reply was, "After you hear what happened to me, you won't."

"What do you mean?" he asked.

I proceeded to tell him about my abusive prior boyfriend and how he tried to rape me. I explained how I got away and how dirty and ashamed I felt.

You see, one night at the age of 17, I shot tequila for the first time and passed out. When I woke up he was fondling me. I was crushed. I stayed in the abusive relationship. I was taught to wait for my husband, and now that he had touched me I thought I had to marry him. It was not long after that night he tried to date-rape me. I escaped and locked myself in the bathroom. At 2:00 a.m. a friend came looking for me and took me home. Needless to say, I broke up with that man and decided that I would not date anyone. I did go out with friends and on some dates, but I would pay for my own meal to avoid any misconceptions that I was looking for a boyfriend. I did not want to fall in love again. Love meant too much pain. After I told Michael all about these events, he looked me in the eyes again and said, "You are the one he was talking about?" He knew my prior boyfriend, and he had told Michael that I wouldn't sleep around.

"Angela, you are still pure, you are still a virgin, and I will wait for you forever. It was not your fault, and I want to marry you. I told God that I wanted a good woman, and to let the next virgin I meet be my wife. I love you."

I told him that I was not in love with him as my heart was still broken and I did not know how long it would take to heal.

Again, he told me, "I will wait for you for forever."

In that moment, my heart melted. I was done searching. Even though I was confused, I had never known such love and I didn't ever want to lose it. My heart was so wounded that I was not sure of any of my feelings that night, except I did not ever want to leave his arms as he held me and I cried. Eighteen months later we were married.

As I mentioned earlier, the weirdest thing that I cannot explain happened. As soon as we arrived in the car to go to our wedding reception, I felt like I was in the car with a complete stranger. He had changed, and it was in an instant. He had shifted from my companion to my god. He hadn't done anything; it was a change in his attitude. When I asked what was wrong, he had no idea that anything had changed. For years we were in the dark to this phenomenon, and we had no idea how to address what he could not see. At times, I am sure he thought that I was being too sensitive or demanding. Today I look back and see how we both believed that he was supposed to be my god but were blind to that reality.

What happened? Where was my boyfriend, my best friend, this man of compassion who had offered total acceptance? From that moment forward, I kept looking for the man I fell in love with but could not find him. Michael had all of a sudden become the man of the house. He began to treat me like I was his daughter, not his wife. He would say things like, "Woman, don't you think you are going to change me," and "Who told you that you could buy that?" and "You did not ask me if you could go there." This was nothing like the man I knew before. The very first week he raised his voice and cursed at me while glaring like he would hurt me.

I stood up tall and looked him in the eyes and told him, "I never saw my daddy speak to my mother this way, and no man will ever speak to me this way. If you want to holler or throw something, that is your business, but it will not be in my presence. If you ever speak to me that way again, you will come home to an empty house." My voice was soft yet firm as I did not raise it to match his. I spoke with an assurance of who I was. To tell the truth, I do not know how I did that, as I was extremely codependent and scared. Little did I know, my troubles had only just begun to be unveiled.

Months passed and through much prayer and soul-searching, I clearly heard God tell me that I needed to return to Him and He would guide me. At age fourteen I had given my life to Jesus. I remember lying in my bed and asking Him to help me and live in me. I didn't really understand what I was saying; I was really scared of going to hell. I wasn't looking for God to take over; I just didn't want to suffer.

At that very moment, I saw a white ball of light come through the east wall of my room and enter into my chest. I fell back on my pillow and with shock sprang up and ran to my mother. She was asleep and in a bit of a stupor said, "That's nice, Honey. Go back to bed."

I couldn't believe it. "That's nice, Honey." I figured that everyone got a ball of light in their chest when God came to live in them. After that, I remember talking to God all the time and He talked to me, just like when I was little girl. After about a year our conversations faded, as I turned to friends and high school activities. I actually had gone five years with very little communication with God. However, now I was in trouble in my marriage and I needed help. Again, I was really looking to escape suffering. I didn't know that God wanted to have relationship with me.

My life was falling apart; I needed help for every second of every day. As I called out, again, I began to hear God in my head and heart. The best way I can explain it is that it was inside my ear but not audible. The voice came in complete thoughts; it came all at once from out of nowhere and it was completely contrary to my way of thinking. I began to dream dreams and have open visions. My memory of Scripture became supernatural. I could read a passage once and remember it, chapter and verse. Moreover, anytime

I needed an answer, I could go look in the Bible and somehow find exactly what I was looking for. Note, I had never studied the Bible before now and I didn't have Google or a concordance. The Spirit of God would lead me. I seemed to live in amazement of all the ways God would speak to me.

Growing up Catholic, I had never really been taught the entire Bible. We studied from the four Gospels and the homily, and I attended catechism classes. One of my teachers actually told me that the Bible was too confusing and that we should only let our teachers and the priest tell us what the Bible was saying.

I can remember the excitement when I heard God tell me that he had called me to be like the prophet Jeremiah. I was so happy. That is, until I went and read the book. Ugh. No! I didn't want to be like that, weeping and rejected. After crying and begging "no," feeling like I really didn't have a choice in the matter, hesitantly, I said OK.

I heard my Father say, "Do you trust Me?"

That felt horrible.

With courage, and fear of my own doubts, I said, "Yes God, I trust You."

With little church experience, and not being versed in the Scriptures, I trusted in the God I spoke to as a child. I remembered playing with God as He made shapes in the clouds just for me. I played hide-and-seek, asking Him to show me where He was hiding in the flowers and such. I never hid from Him, though, as I knew He could see me wherever I was. He comforted me at night, when I was scared of the dark, and I slept with my Bible under my pillow. He seemed like a faraway grandfather I could trust, but who would correct me when need be. I pretty much saw God like I saw my Paw-Paw. Paw-Paw Lea lived with us and he was my best friend. He was nice, playful, stern, and protective. We didn't go to church much, so I had not yet been taught to be afraid of the devil or God. Therefore, my fears were more along the lines of disappointing or disobeying God.

Now I went crying to God daily about my husband, and daily he would tell me that Michael's problems were between Him and Michael. Father would tell me that we were going to work in my heart. "I am not the one who is mean," was my reply, and I did not think that I was the one who had issues. I was convinced that if Michael would seek God the way I was and if he would start serving God like me, then we would be OK. I could not understand why God would not let me work on Michael's issues.

Moreover, every time I did complain, God would listen and validate me. The only problem was He would tell me that I was doing the same thing to Jesus that Michael was doing to me. What? How was that possible? I did not understand God my Father, God the Holy Spirit, and Jesus very well. When I prayed, I never quite knew which one I was talking to. God showed me that I came to Him looking for a savior and Jesus had restored me to Him, my Father. He also showed me that the Holy Spirit was my teacher and my comforter, but that Jesus wanted to be the lover of my soul. To be honest, that sounded a little bit creepy to me at the time. How was Jesus going to be my husband, and what did "lover of my soul" mean? I was not sure that I could wrap my mind around that thought, because I was nineteen and a newlywed. I was reluctant, but I opened my heart and asked God to teach me. Jesus was my provider, protector, and the giver of all good gifts in my life. He was the one who would make me feel complete and give me abundant life.

It wasn't long until I began to understand that I had put Michael in the place of God. I was attempting to find my value and identity in him. I wanted him to make me feel needed, wanted, pretty, desirable, smart, worthy, and accepted. I had placed on him the responsibility of making me into a whole person. Lacking understanding, I wanted him to heal my heart and soul.

When he failed, I wanted God to fix him. What I quickly came to understand is that God was healing me, and Michael could not fill God's shoes.

Had my husband possessed the ability to give me these things, I would not have sought God. I would have settled for what man could substitute, and then he would be damned to keep up the good works to avoid suffering the consequences of a discontented wife. Today I am very grateful for his presumed failures. The truth of the matter is, his failures were just what I needed to heal me. Through these painful transitions, I learned that God is the only one who could make me whole.

Healthy relationships with anyone start with a healthy heart and mind. When I began to rely on God to fulfill *all* of my needs, everything changed. It was very hard and I spent a lot of time crying out to God, often on my face or in my closet on the floor. Waiting for some kind of direction or answers was lonely and often seemed to take forever. This was the beginning of finding my self-worth, security, peace, and joy.

I had spent my entire life receiving love and acceptance by being good, and that was the foundation on which I had established my self-worth and self-acceptance. You see, being the fifth out of six girls, I learned how to *not* get a spanking. I learned to keep my room clean, my clothes washed, my homework done, and my grades on the honor roll. I measured love by my works and being "good." However, if you had asked me if this was my value system, I would have told you "no way." It wasn't long after studying the Bible and attending church that I could answer all of the spiritual questions with the correct biblical answers. I held—and still hold—the Word of God in the highest regard, believing it to be all truth. The subtle deception is that I also believed that I was an obedient, good Christian. I was living in denial.

Using this as my measuring tool against my own self, I was also subconsciously using it against others, but I was not aware that this was even in my belief system. To put it in simple terms, I was doing good in my marriage expecting my husband to repay me with good. My life was a trade system, and I was not aware of how deeply this had grown in my heart and soul. I was looking outside of myself to get joy and love. I was working hard and expecting my husband to do the same. I read that to be friends with the world meant to be God's enemy and those who did this were even called "adulterers and adulteresses." Ugh. I hated adultery. I wanted to make sure I did not do this, so I kept looking for what *to do.* God was speaking to me and telling me that to seek affirmation outside of Him and to get fulfillment from any other source was seeking the pleasures of the world. Now I want you to understand, I was not out doing bad things. I was simply seeking to get my self-worth and happiness through my husband, outside of God, and this is what God was showing me. I was very confused, because I thought being good was what God wanted from me. Moreover, I thought being of the "world" meant doing bad things like stealing or murder.

After I read the Scripture "But seek ye first His kingdom, and His righteousness; and all these things shall be added unto you" (Matthew 6:33 ASV), I endeavored to obey this. After all, I wanted everything added to me. I understood this to mean read my bible, pray, go to church, give tithes, give offerings, take care of others, do good and do not do evil, and spend time worshiping and praising God. I was now on my way to peace and joy and happiness, or so I thought.

I was raised to be good and obedient, so this was my pathway to God. I learned the Word and began my attempt to "do" it and obey. It was what I needed at the time. Scripture tells us that a child and a slave are treated the same, even though the child is master of all. What did that mean? Basically, both the child and the slave are told "Go here and not there, eat this and not that, touch this and don't touch that." It is all about the rules and obedience. So as a child of faith, that is what I did. My relationship was a father/ daughter relationship, and I was going to be the best daughter I could be. God's faithfulness abounded and He showed Himself to me daily. I wanted to know Him and what He expected of me, and then I wanted to do whatever that was. No cost was too high for me. After all, that is how I would get His love and approval. I had forgotten about Jesus being the "lover of my soul." Besides, that sounded weird anyway.

There were times when I would be so tired of obeying God. I would tell Him, "If my husband would just do this, then I will do that."

God so gently replied, "So if Michael doesn't comply, you are going to disobey and do whatever you want? How will that work for Me and you?"

Quickly I learned that no matter what anyone did, I wanted my Father's approval more than anyone or anything. For the time being, and in my healing from codependency, this was what I needed. However, it wouldn't be long and that too would transition.

I became more confused. *Oh God! Does this mean that I must be a doormat Christian?* I did not understand how to deal with the faults of others and obey God and not let others abuse or disrespect me. For a codependent person, this felt like insanity. When I asked God for direction He led me to the letters to the churches in the book of Revelations. I read them and began to write letters to Michael as I patterned them after the way God wrote to the seven churches.

Studying these letters, I noticed how God would first encourage the churches by telling them what blessed His heart. He would express His love, gratitude, and His faithfulness to them. Only then would He bring up the things that hurt His heart. He explained the problem in detail with gentleness, and then

No Longer Dis-Eve'd

He would offer a solution to their problem, all the while bringing to their remembrance the place where their relationship was wounded. He made clear in the letters His desire for unity. In addition, He gave them the freedom to walk away from the relationship if they were not able to comply. It was always evident that His heart was to restore the relationship. Finally, He would end the letter describing what their restored relationship could be in the everlasting blessed relationship in the paradise of God.

God gave me the art of letter-writing because talking with Michael did not work for us. I would start out with an issue that I felt was an injustice and before I knew what was happening, I was apologizing and left feeling empty like a failure. Michael would divert from the topic, finding any place where I had wounded him. I would relent in my desire for unity, yet I remained hopeless and confused as to what and how that happened. Learning to write letters took me out of the codependent behavior and allowed me to state my heart simply and clearly. There was no room for manipulation, nor for me to crumble or grovel for love and acceptance. This approach allowed me to find my voice as opposed to crying like a victim in my dysfunctional self-worth.

I was not skilled at expressing my feelings in a healthy manner. I would run from any anger, mine or his. My feelings would cloud my thoughts and I would shut down. I could not figure out how he could get me to accept the responsibility for his disrespect, neglect, or anger. When I didn't shut down, I would become pushy and insistent on my way.

Where did our extreme dysfunction come from, and was there a remedy? In my studies, I noticed a pattern and I named it "The Adam Disease." It is a disease in the land of dust, the land of our borders.

Eve ate and saw it was good, and then gave it to Adam. Adam ate and they saw they were naked. They covered, ran, and hid. Then they blamed others and were separated from God. So here are the symptoms. We eat an experience and digest it to determine if the situation is good or bad. Then, after we make our determination, we cover up our issues, then we run from our feelings and each other, and then we blame each other. If that doesn't work, we will blame God and then pull away from Him by withdrawing from communion. Thereby we separate our own hearts from each other and our relationships die.

Writing letters helped me to not cover up, not run, and not hide. It gave me a safe place to seek God without the fear of being blamed. It was a way for us to speak and listen to each other. You see, we both treasured our marriage and we were in love with each other. Neither of us knew what to do with our emotions, nor how to express them in a healthy manner. In our attempt to escape our sorrow and sufferings, we would do whatever we could in the heat of the moment, and often that was not healthy.

Confrontation is necessary in all relationships, but we must be able to both confront and be confronted. This is crazy hard for a codependent who often smothers their partner. It is just as painful for an angry person who prefers to isolate. The angry person just wants to be left alone in hopes it will all go away. Fear becomes a method to prevent the codependent from getting too close. Unfortunately for the angry person, they usually get the blame for being mean or rude. Both parties are guilty of being broken.

Let's look at a dysfunction this way. Let's pretend that someone accidentally spits in your face by sneezing or while they were talking. Let's assume it was obviously an accident. This would not be a problem even though it is not a desired situation for the recipient. Moreover, the delivery person may even suffer embarrassment and express their sorrow. All is good, no conflict necessary. Now let's say this same person gets some sort of perverted joy from spitting on people. Let's say that this person persists in spitting on you every time they see you face to face. The first time it could easily appear as an accident. The second time, you may say something like, "Back up, please, or cover your mouth; you are spitting on me."

However, by the third time you are realizing that this person is either mentally incapable of comprehension or maybe physically handicapped.

If neither of these exist, then confrontation is necessary. If that doesn't resolve the situation, the next step could be that this person no longer gets the luxury of your presence. You see, we must respect ourselves or others will not. To allow others to disrespect us is not loving ourselves. We will only love others based on how we perceive that we are loved by our heavenly Father. When we know, feel, and understand how much we are loved, then we live our relationships out of this understanding from a subconscious and a conscious level. This prevents us from trading goodness for love and acceptance—as if love could be earned.

No Longer Dis-Eve'd

In marriage, it is not only necessary that we respect each other, but we must also have self-respect. Moreover, the marriage union must be cherished. When our hearts are aware that we are already loved and our marriage is a gift to unite us in that love, our responses then flow from that understanding. We are no longer bound by the illusion that love can be earned or traded, for God is love.

As I started to rely on God as my source, He began to ask me questions like, "What is best for the union?" Wow; I was given permission to protect the marriage by respecting myself and him. You mean I did not have to be a doormat and accept abuse? Absolutely not. On the contrary, to allow abuse of any kind would destroy the marriage, and I had vowed to honor our union. Isolating and smothering were both dishonoring to our marriage union, for they both were detrimental.

Respect was a key factor. Respect was the very thing that required me to let go of all control and manipulation. I had been using control and manipulation in my attempts to get my husband to meet my needs and fulfill my expectations. This was not healthy or loving.

Having the need to control myself or others was based out of fear—often, the fear of rejection. Perfect love has no need for fear of any kind. Giving up control meant I had to trust in love, and I was not sure how to love. I did not understand at the time that God is love and that love is the result of my union with God. I was still of the opinion that love was the list of things that I needed to do to show my love. Moreover, that meant that I only felt love if Michael did what I expected him to do to show love.

Oh my, how hopeless did this seem at times! The concept that love is a person, not an action, made no sense at first. Now, I am free, and love does what I am not able to do. For God truly lives through us and is accomplishing it all. We are the joyous recipients who, without self-effort, receive all by way of promise.

It was time to start learning how to trust God and how to receive His love. This was a pretty big deal, as my idea of love was built on duty. I could not rely on myself to fix the problems. But oh, how I tried. I tried so much and for so long, until I was fully persuaded that I was not able. The more I tried, the more I seemed to get into trouble.

Angela Bertone

All along, God simply wanted to heal my wounded heart and remove all my fears. He would gently and patiently do this by revealing to me how much He loved me. It did not matter what He had to do or how long it would take, **He would wait for me for forever if I needed it.** That reminded me of the very words that Michael said that night he melted my heart and I cried in his arms.

One night, as Michael slept, I stared into the darkness while the bones in my chest ached with sorrow and grief. I thought to myself, "Our marriage is falling apart! How can you sleep?" It appeared that he was oblivious to my pain. From my side of the bed, with a great gulf between us, I cried out to God. "How can he sleep, while my heart breaks?"

We had gone around the same mountain again, only to regurgitate the familiar apologies with no lasting change. I heard Jesus say to me, "Come meet Me in the green room." I arose with my cry-baby pillow and blanket, feeling sorry for myself, and curled up on the sofa sobbing. "Open your eyes," I heard Him say. To my surprise, I looked and saw Jesus standing before me. To my left was a large boulder where three men leaned, sleeping. Jesus' face was streaming with a mixtures of tears, blood, and sweat. His garments were becoming soaked and He appeared to have the weight of the world on His shoulders. "Every time you felt alone, crying out to Father, and it appeared that He could not be found, I was here waiting for you. I knew you would make it. Father and I believed in you. Before time, I saw you suffering while Michael slept, and I told My Father, when I cry out, even if I sweat blood, don't answer Me. **I must drink from her cup and eat from her brokenness!**" He took me into the garden and together we wept. While Michael slept in the other room I watched Jesus' disciples sleeping as I looked through the brush. Leaning on His heart, Jesus explained to me that every sorrow and suffering that I would ever face, He had faced before time. He invited me to suffer with Him.

"Are you greater than Me, Angela?"

"No Jesus, why would You ask me that?"

"You expect Father to deliver you from your sorrow and suffering, but you claim to be one with Me. How can you know Me intimately if Father delivers you from your pain, while He required Me to suffer? Are you willing to follow Me?"

"Yes, Jesus, I am willing. I would lay my life down for You."

"Then you must take the same path as Me. You too shall be rejected, forsaken, betrayed, falsely accused, and help others while at the same time not be able to help yourself. Many will question you and even say that the works you do are of Beelzebub. Are you sure you want to follow Me?"

"Will it be my husband who betrays me?"

With no response to my question, again He asked, "Will you follow Me? If it cost you your life, will you follow Me?"

Brokenhearted and afraid, I replied, "Yes, I will follow You."

I had no idea the depths of His request, nor did my mind want to think about it. All I really knew after such an encounter was that I could trust Him and He would never leave me. This night changed my life, and the sorrows that I was experiencing paled compared to the suffering I saw in His eyes that night. This was the first time ever that I had actually understood what it meant to eat of His broken body and drink from the cup of His suffering. It was as though I had been given a new set of eyes and ears.

Are you tired yet? How long have you traded love for love, and is it working? I have heard that doing the same thing over and over expecting different results is…well, you know, crazy.

Chapter 7: Respect for Myself and Others

We are the temples of God. Jesus was angry when the religious leaders made His Father's house a den of thieves. They had set up tables of exchange. This appeared to be for convenience, as it was the law to sacrifice in the temple. Yet Jesus knew the hearts of the people and was heartbroken because His Father's house was to be a place for relationship and communion, not a place of trade.

This is the very thing I had done in my marriage. I wanted to be good to show my love so that Michael would feel love, and I wanted Michael to be good so I would feel his love. This is a trade mentality.

Jesus actions and anger showed this mentality was unacceptable, no matter the excuse or the law. It was a wakeup call again. My heart had become a place of trade and expectations. It was now time for my heart to be cleansed from such putrid thinking.

I was in so much denial that I needed the conviction and guilt to open my eyes in the middle of my trading in order to see. This was very humbling. It required me to go to Michael often and tell him that my efforts were to control and manipulate, and that I was sorry. I would ask for forgiveness and let go of all of my expectations. For example, I had placed the expectation on him to buy me gifts on certain holidays. Sometimes he would and sometimes he wouldn't. If not, I would pout and complain because he did not measure up to my expectation. Let's get honest. If I wanted him to give me something because it was the right thing to do, but he had no desire to do it, why would I want it?

The reason is, I had bought into the idea that if he loved me, then he would do these traditional things. Had I not understood that it is traditions that make the Word of God have no effect? It was becoming clear to me the reason

95

Jesus did not want the basis of our relationship to be traditions. Did I want traditions or passion?

In my lack of intimacy, I wanted him to want to do things, and got mad when he did not want to. How nutty is that? That is sort of like getting mad if I made broccoli and he did not eat it because he didn't like it. I wanted to change his taste buds. This was so hard. What would others think if my husband did not buy me these traditional gifts? I would be embarrassed. Fear of what others would think was one of the underlying factors that made me want him to comply with the traditions. Jesus was showing me that traditions were robbing us of passionate intimacy and a healthy marriage.

I found it hypocritical that I taught women that making love as a wifely duty was detestable, yet I was expecting Michael to comply with traditional husband duties. What a prideful double standard!

It became evident that anything and everything that I judged him for, I was doing. "Judge not, that ye be not judged. For with what judgment ye judge, ye shall be judged: and with what measure ye mete, it shall be measured unto you" (Matthew 7:1-2 ASV). Sigh…

Sometimes the teachings under which I had submitted myself enabled me to blame others for my problems. This was not my intent, nor do I think it was the intent of my leaders. However, God was showing me that our judgment of others was setting us up for the same cycle. Judgment is in our nature as a result of what Adam and Eve ate in the garden. It is the outworking of our dependence on our knowledge of good and evil. This knowledge makes us judges in our very nature. That is why Jesus said He did not come to condemn us but to set us free. He was not warning us to avoid judgment. Nor was it given like a commandment—thou shall not judge. He was explaining to us our fallen condition.

God's grace and wisdom gifted us our physical senses—sight, smell, taste, touch, and hearing. These physical senses are our communication system of the physical body, and they help us to judge continually. In addition, they are created things that teach us about the unseen senses of our heart. Romans 1:20 teaches us that everything that is created reveals that which is unseen, including the Godhead and His eternal power.

Angela Bertone

Pain is sensed in our senses. It communicates to us something about our condition or our surroundings. It is vital to our survival that we have the ability to interpret why and where the pain is coming from. This is to protect us from harm. Likewise, the spiritual senses do the same for us. However, we do not like to experience pain. We need to expand our understanding of why we have the senses. They are not just to protect us but are a form of communication. As the physical senses communicate with our bodies, likewise the spiritual senses are God's way to communicate to our spirits. This takes place in the heart though the emotions.

All that is needed for us to fail in the area of communication is to discredit the emotions as some fleshly physical response that we need to control, thereby denying the power of God that abides in us as a form of communication. Ezekiel 36:25 tells us this is so. A hard heart is all that is necessary to keep us from an intimate relationship with God and others. If we cannot be intimate with the one we can see and the one we are physically married to, how can we be intimate with Jesus whom we cannot see yet are supposed to be married to? Jesus rebuked His disciples for their calloused hearts when they did not understand the miracle of the bread and feeding of the multitude. He referred to Isaiah and remarked "truly he prophesied well," noting the people could not see nor hear. The religious leaders were indignant and asked Jesus if He was accusing them of being blind.

I can almost hear Him now asking us, "Is your heart still hard, do you still not see? Is your heart still hard, do you still not hear?" To go past our feelings, as discussed in the fourth chapter of Ephesians, is all that is necessary to miss the mark and enter into all manner of evil. In so doing we are then giving ourselves over to all manner of lasciviousness, which includes wantonness, lack, mercilessness, lust, and greed. Emotions are eternal and the logical mind calculates based on our limited understanding that has been formed by our past experiences and education. Going past our feelings and failing to lift them up to God, along with our corrupted opinion and judgments, we will be trapped by our judgments and then dammed to receive the same in judgment in return. Our emotional pain offers us the opportunity to seek God's face and hear His voice about our every circumstance. It is in this yielded state that God gives us grace.

No Longer Dis-Eve'd

If our skin could not feel, we would call it dead or callused. These are two more words used by Jesus to describe mankind—calloused hearts and dead in our trespasses and sin. Why did He call them dead? Could it be the same reason that we call something dead? For instance, when a body is still alive yet all of the senses no longer work, we would call them brain dead. When we go to the dentist and they give us a shot of Novocain, the doctor will ask, "Is it dead yet?" He is asking if you can "feel" any sensations. If the answer is no, then we call it dead.

So here it is again. To be dead is not to feel. This is why God promised to take out our hearts of stone (ones that cannot feel) and give us a heart of flesh (one that can feel) and fill it with His Spirit; and He would cause us to walk in His statutes and ye shall keep His judgments and do them. Why did He use the words "cause," "shall," and "do"? Because the will of man is not able to walk in God's statutes nor keep His commandments.

Scripture makes it clear that apart from God we can do nothing, and our best efforts are as filthy rags. In fact, Paul wrote this: "For I know that in me (that is, in my flesh) dwelleth no good thing: for to will is present with me; but how to perform that which is good I find not" (Romans 7:18 KJV; emphasis mine). The phrase "to will" here is the Greek word *thelō ethelō* and denotes "to choose, to prefer, to wish, and to be inclined for the future as in to be about to." Moreover, it denotes "desire, intent, will, and willing." On the other hand, the terms "cause you, ye shall keep, and do aforementioned in the promise" are the Hebrew words cause[8], ye shall keep[9], and do[10], all indicating that God is accomplishing, executing, hedging, guarding and protecting as an observant watchman. There is no indication that man is helping God or assisting God, but rather God alone is causing us to accomplish and He alone is guarding over us like a hedge.

Why did He use the word *shall* and not *will*? Because the will is not able to walk in God's statutes nor keep His commandments. That is why it is by way of promise and not obedience in the traditional sense of the English word. The Hebrew word for "shall" here is *asah* (aw-saw), which means to make you, to cause you, to bring forth. God was declaring that He would do what

---

8. Strongs H6213.
9. Strongs H8104.
10. Strongs H6213.

man was not able to do. The word "walk" here is *halak* (haw-lak), and it also means to be conversant, to grow, to enter, and it is from the word *yalak* (yaw-lak), and it means to walk and carry, bear, bring, to come away with. These indicate unity, as in together with God, not for God.

Our calloused hearts were the precise reason that neither Michael nor I could do enough to make our marriage work, nor could we make each other happy or feel loved. These feelings do not come as a result of man's efforts. They come as a result of God fulfilling His promises in us and through us. God actually gave man the promise as He declared that He would sanctify His name that His children had profaned. You can read about it in Ezekiel 36:23.

What does this have to do with the temple of trades, the judgments, and pain? Using our hearts as a place of trade brings about disappointment, and then we judge and blame each other, causing each other emotional pain. Then we run from what we perceive as our source of pain, which is often each other. Then we become divided and our marriages begin to fail.

Our hearts that have become like stones in our efforts to become pain-free are too calloused to hear God, and like Adam and Eve we have left our ability to communicate with God as a result of our calloused hearts. That is why God promised to take them out and give us a new heart of flesh—one that could feel again. After that, He promised to fill it with His Spirit. This is the life-giving Spirit of Jesus who was called the last Adam, talked about in 1 Corinthians. "It is sown a natural body; it is raised a spiritual body. If there is a natural body, there is also a spiritual body. So also, it is written, the first man Adam became a living soul. The last Adam became a life-giving spirit. Howbeit that is not first which is spiritual, but that which is natural; then that which is spiritual" (1 Corinthians 15:44-46 ASV, emphasis mine*)*. Note again we see Adam (natural) is a receiver and Jesus (spiritual) is a giver. Again, we are seeing how the two become one. This is where our marriage to Jesus actually takes place. We must realize that we have nothing to give unless it is first received in our natural brain, and then after it dies in our inability to perform it Jesus resurrects it to life in and through us.

Relationship is only found and can only live in the union of intimacy. "Intimacy" is the word *yada* in Hebrew. It is the same word used when Adam knew Eve and she bore a son. It is the word used for intercourse. Inside of the word *yada* are the words "understanding, respect, honor." We can only understand someone intimately if we have felt the same feelings. Let's take the death of a child for example. If your child has died but mine is still living, is it possible for me to understand or to "know" you? No. Most definitely not. And if someone is foolish and says they do understand, it will incite anger in the parent who has buried a child. To feel is to understand. This is done with the emotions. It is not possible to kill only some emotions and keep others alive. The heart either becomes calloused or it is tender.

The word *understand* means "to feel" and to feel means to "turn." When one feels extreme heat from being in close proximity with fire, he will "turn" as a result of the heat that was felt. The feelings are those which cause us to turn. This is also true with our emotional feelings. They will cause us to turn toward or away from each other to feel pleasure and to avoid pain.

Jesus said to remember Him. What was He speaking of? The word *remember* is the same word as intimacy and intercourse. It actually means husband or farmer—one who plants seeds. We realize that all intimacy is not intercourse and there are different levels of intimacy. Let's take a look at sexual intimacy and observe the actual word *intercourse*. It can be looked at like this—*inter,* or to enter into, and *course,* or chorus. We can see in the word *intercourse* is the union of two voices that enter into the same heart where the voices come into unity, like the voices in a chorus. In order to meet the definition of a chorus they must sing in unison.

The unison of the emotions transcends both space and time and can exist in all places at the same time. When both hearts feel the same or feel understood by each other, intimacy is experienced.

Hearts are united only by the emotions. Therefore, we can have unity in rejoicing and weeping. That is why Jesus said weep with those who weep and rejoice with those who rejoice. This is unity—just another dimension of it.

That is how we can *"be one"* with God and with each other. We know that the physical sexual intimacy between the man and woman in marriage is an allegorical mystery to reveal our intimacy with God. The physical is only a created thing that unveils the unseen or heart intimacy, for heart intimacy is eternal. Scientists have confirmed that the emotions respond and entangle quantumly. This can be understood by the "twin-atom beam" experiment, by Robert Bucker, and Dr. Pavel Naumov's mother rabbit experiment. We can now observe science that explains what the Bible has said all along.

In the "twin-atom beam" experiment, a single light particle was divided into two photons. They were separated fourteen miles apart. The goal was to expose one photon to change and see if that change affected the photon fourteen miles away, and, if so, how long would it take to be affected. The findings were astonishing. As one photon was introduced to different stimuli, the second photon responded exactly the same way, and without delay, as the photon being manipulated. This was evidence of their electric and magnetic entanglement. Moreover, space and time did not play a factor. In the rabbit experiment, a mother rabbit was separated from her babies by water, space, and time. While underwater in a submarine, the baby rabbits were tortured and then killed one by one. The mother was being monitored with an implanted EEG in her brain to measure the effects if any as each of her babies experienced pain. Simultaneously, as each baby was killed the mother's brain produced detectable recordable reactions, showing no delay in time, even though they were separated by distance, depth, and water. Tests like these support that the modern day quantum physics studies that give evidence that our emotions are not bound by space or time. Ecclesiastes states that eternity is inside of us in our hearts.

Our physical and emotional senses communicate within the body and cause the body to respond without the need of logic or another person's instructions. Pain will do that for us. This is also true of a foul odor. If I held a piece of rotten meat on a fork and attempted to eat it, my nose would tell me not to. I would not need another person to tell me what to do so that I could choose to obey or not. The sense of smell would do that for me instinctively. If the senses did not work then we would have a problem. This is the same kind of response our hearts would have if they were healed.

Only those who exercise the spiritual senses are able to eat and chew and swallow and digest and receive nutrients from spiritual meat. Long ago we as Christians should have been off milk, and we should even be teaching others. We must examine our hearts. We must ask God to take out our hearts of stone and to cause our hearts to feel again. If it costs us everything we must have understanding. Understanding comes in the emotions of the heart—a heart of flesh that is filled with the Spirit of God.

We are told that if we seek the *heart* then we would have the mind of the Holy Spirit. God draws close to us when we are of a broken and contrite heart, and Jesus is the King of the brokenhearted. The Bible tells us that the Word of God comes first to the Jew (inside the broken heart) and then to the Greek (language/intellect).

It is after our hearts become tender and sensitive that we can not only feel our pain, but we can now gain understanding. We can respect ourselves and one another only after God has healed our hearts and made us one with His heart. The act of seeking understanding will bring us to a place of compassion. This is what we are all looking for when we have been wounded or abused.

Our past wounds and the perceptions that have formed our belief system are held in our heart-brain and need healing. Only after we have grown weary from our wounds and our fruitless desire for revenge will we seek help. After we have found our identity in Christ, we are more likely to seek His face and see where He suffered the same sorrowful situation. Only then can we understand the very things that appeared to be against us are being used by God to reveal His love. His love alone can transform us from fearful to loved in every situation.

What does this look like? I remember one night I was wounded and complaining to God because I was feeling lonely. Once again, Michael had not met my expectations. I wanted him to spend time with me on weekends, just like we did before marriage. Therefore, I would plan in my head how the weekend would look:

Ah! Friday. He will come home from work and we will sit down and have a nice dinner together. We will cuddle and talk and maybe play a game or take a walk. Then we will spend the evening watching a movie while he holds me in his arms.

Actually, it went more like this: Friday, 5:00 p.m., he drove up in the driveway. I met him at the door and served him a hot supper. He went outside and worked in the yard till dark. Then he took his bath and retired in the living room to watch a bliss-filled night of football for hours until he fell asleep. Ugh!

He never spends any time with me. He is too busy or watching TV. Does he love me? Oh God! Help! I am lonely.

He would spend all his time with me when we were dating. *What happened? What did I do? He only comes to me when he wants something.* Looking back at myself, I can say, "Poor little victim, no wonder he wanted to escape. Yuck!"

While I whined, the Lord would say so softly and tenderly, "I know, Angela, I feel the same way with you." My heart sank, as I knew it was true. I only spent time with God so I could learn how to do good and do what He wanted, so He would bless me and give me what I wanted in my marriage. How could I be so blind? Truly we do reap what we sow. I was doing to God the very thing I was complaining to Him about—accusing Michael of not loving me anymore.

This realization began to cause some drastic changes in me. To feel the pain that I was causing God was like getting too close to the fire, and it was turning me away from my selfish, codependent victim needs to the One who created me. It did not seem to matter what I was feeling; God understood. Usually it was me who caused God such pain. If I am made in God's likeness and image, then His heart is the one mine is patterned after.

After all, the Bible tells us that God grieved for forty years while His children wandered and did not enter into the Promised Land. The Holy Spirit can be grieved, and we are exhorted not to grieve the Holy Spirit. Every time Jesus healed someone, He had compassion on them. God's heart is described as tender and compassionate, and He draws close to the brokenhearted. How could we as a society be so against our own emotions and expect to have deep, lasting relationships?

In time, I began to desire to know God's heart intimately. I found that in my sorrow and suffering His heart was revealed and my heart began to melt. God is love, and He is not conditional. He will not enable me to disrespect myself or others. Moreover, He instructs me so that I do not walk in destructive, controlling, or manipulative behavior without pain. The pain is my barometer to direct my path.

I began to learn to speak the truth in love, to express my commitment of love, and to accept others and keep a balanced life. Holding people accountable is very difficult when you have a codependent past, as it is easy to step back into the fear of rejection and self-pity. Man's approval must fall away to heal from this condition. Codependency will destroy relationships and can often be a long and drawn out misery for everyone involved.

I learned to make my requests known and let my "yes be yes" and my "no be no." In so doing, I learned to accept others who said yes and no. I did not need to control them anymore. I understand that some will reject me, yet I am not moved by their opinions of me. Moreover, I now understand that any division also brings with it multiplication. This truth sets me free, and I can rejoice at the harvest that is disguised in the division. I rest in knowing that God never rejects me and is always for me. He even made all of creation that way. All things are from God, for God, and return to God. I am made in that same image. Therefore, everything is from me, for me, and back to me. No weapon of any kind can effectively be against me; moreover, even if it was God will turn it for my good. These truths cause me to see others very differently, and fear cannot abide in me. Note: I knew in my logic that God loved me and was for me, and I could quote the Scriptures chapter and verse, but it was not until my heart-brain emotional feelings were healed that my life became spontaneously abundant. Even if we believe one hundred percent with our head knowledge but feel alone, rejected, abandoned, then our head knowledge will keep us dis-Eve'd and not living the abundant life.

In addition, I no longer had the need to fix others (especially my husband). I began to learn to seek and know a person's heart. By seeking understanding, I could hear God and get direction. Marriage afforded me lots of practice. I began to see that he is my gift. He is worth fighting for. I was not willing any longer to fight to be right; however, I would fight for our unity and passion. Divorce was not an option for me. If Michael ever wanted it, I was not able to control that. I learned to let go of everything—even what he wanted. I knew freedom is what love gives, because that is what God gave me. So, if Michael ever wanted out of our marriage, that would be his decision. I no longer needed, nor wanted, to have a begging mentality; how disgusting, anyway.

When God would ask me to serve Michael and I was wounded, I thought it would kill me at first. In addition, God required me to confront issues when I was weak and often afraid. This kind of pain made me determined to find truth. I became desperate to hear God's voice and would do nothing until I had instructions from the Holy Spirit. Anytime I reverted back to my codependent behavior, our relationship got worse, causing more pain. And it was pain that kept me on my face seeking for answers. I learned that God is

faithful and He would always show me what to say or do at just the perfect time. He was always for me and never against me.

There were times when God did not answer me for weeks. To tell the truth, a few times I felt like I would lose my mind. I now know that God was forming in me patience and temperance to endure things I would face in my future. How clear is hindsight? Looking back, I am so grateful for those long waits. Today they give me peace and comfort in hard times.

You know, seeking the kingdom is nothing like I thought it was. Seeking the kingdom is not in what I did, but it was in going deep into my heart where all the pain existed and finding God there waiting to show me His love. In finding His love, my life was—and is—transformed from fear to perfect love.

Are you living abundantly? Are all things being added unto you? Do you have righteousness, peace, and joy? If not, take heart. Michael and I can testify that the pathway into our own hearts and the heart of God creates the path for all other intimacy. Marriage is truly the mystery that reveals the love of Jesus for His beloved bride. Let us journey on as we give away to you what God has so freely given unto us.

Chapter 8: Seeking the Kingdom

W here is the kingdom that you are seeking? Is it in the Bible, the church system, scheduled prayers, Sunday school, or acts of kindness? Can it be found in giving, worshiping, reading, or any other activity? Jesus said the Kingdom of God is inside us, in our hearts. If this Kingdom is on the inside, how are we going to discover it by doing actions outside of ourselves? When I ask this question of others, their answers are as follows: read the Bible, go to church, pray, worship, do good, abstain from evil, obey, and give.

If this was the path, why didn't Jesus just give us a list of things to do? That seems easy enough. Jesus, however, had some things to say about the people who trusted in the law and their actions, including the ones given by Moses in the law and the Torah. He used words like pit-vipers, white-washed tombs, thieves, blind guides, and hypocrites. Have you ever wondered why Jesus did not stone the woman they threw at His feet after she was caught in adultery? According to the law of Moses, Jesus should have stoned her. Moreover, He picked corn on the Sabbath and encouraged His disciples to do the same. He did not fast according to custom and neither did His disciples. Moreover, because zeal for His father's house had eaten Him up, He went into the temple and turned over their tables. By traditional accounts in our day, and I assume for those in His day as well, He could have been accused of being *out of control.*

"And in like manner the Spirit also helpeth our infirmity: for we know not how to pray as we ought; but the Spirit himself maketh intercession for us with groanings which cannot be uttered; and he that searcheth the hearts knoweth what is the mind of the Spirit, because he maketh intercession for the saints according to the will of God" (Romans 8:26-27 ASV). Notice in this text there is a clue on how to know the mind of God. It is He who searches the hearts who knows the mind of the Spirit. Isn't that where Jesus told us the Kingdom is?

Am I telling you that to seek the Kingdom of God is to search the hearts of people, including myself? Yes! This is exactly what I am saying. The Word of God is clear on this matter. I know it sounds simple, but trust me—it is not as easy as it sounds. Pain often causes us to run or defend our position. If truth were not painful, we would love it and God would not give us over to a strong delusion as spoken of in 2 Thessalonians 2:10-11.

I have had some rebuttal to this reference, where the argument was that only Jesus can search another person's heart. I agree, yet with Christ all things are possible, and if He is the source-vine and we abide in Him, the flow of revelation as we seek the heart will sprout out of us like a bud in the springtime.

Is it possible to love others if we don't feel loved ourselves by God? I propose that God's Word says we will love as we are loved. God loves us perfectly, yet if we are blind to how much He loves us, then we are not walking in perfect love, and that will produce fear in us. Fear will cause us to need control of our emotions and therefore our circumstances. Often, we attempt this though justification, minimization, and rationalization. These are the mechanisms we use to defend our intellectual understanding of life and the Bible. In so doing we become unknowingly self-righteous.

We are only able to love because He first loved us. Remember the greatest command is to love God with our entire being? If God is love, how can we do love as an action? Is it possible for me to never keep account of a wrong done to me? I have tried to accomplish this task with no success. I have often been stuck in unforgiveness, even when I desire to forgive with my whole being.

How can we know if we are walking in this kind of love? The answer is, if we are free from fear and doubt. This would be the definition of faith, which is full persuasion. Full persuasion occurs in the heart, not the head, because spiritual matters cannot be comprehended with the mind. Moreover, it must be felt with the heart. Only then will the darkness of the unknown be dissolved and the light of His love overtake us, dissipating all fear. It is true that perfect love will destroy all fear, not part of it.

It is not possible for us to seek another person's heart to know it if we are still running from what is inside of our own heart. This is a prerequisite to understanding others. Think about it—how can we see and know another's face if we are too blind or scared to look at our own? After we have gone deep into our own hearts, we will discover the depths of our darkness and, therefore, also see the greatness of His love. Without seeing the darkness, we will deceive ourselves into thinking the love He bestows upon us is because of our goodness. This is a strong delusion.

Were you aware that the oil of myrrh means bitter weeping? It is a cleanser and has healing properties. It was given to Jesus by the wise men along with frankincense and gold. One of the meanings of the word *Frank* means truth. Frankincense represents the aroma of truth. When we face, or smell, our truth, we will weep bitterly. Truth and bitter weeping come together. This produces godly sorrow and creates in us a pure heart. Hence the gold. It is representative of shining, of glory, and of purity. Only the pure in heart can see God.

Once we have experienced every measure of pain in our own hearts without running from it and then experience the resurrection love of Jesus, we are well prepared to seek the hearts of others.

If our senses are not exercised in this manner, we will run or, even worse, try to rescue others from the very thing needed to reveal the love of God in their hearts emotionally.

In the book of Ezekiel, we are promised that God would take out our heart of stone and give us one of flesh. Why would He give us a heart of flesh if flesh was bad? He then said He would fill it with His Spirit and then there was a promise that followed. He promised that we "shall" walk in His statutes and keep His commandments. This promise is not dependent upon our obedience or choices. It is solely a gift from God by way of a *promise*. He is faithful to do what we are not able to do, and it shall be done in the heart and through the heart. So why would God use something that is so deceitfully wicked to lead us by?

Darkness is the place where seeds are supposed to be planted. They are supposed to die and then bring forth fruit. This is the way God created all life. When we ate from the knowledge tree, our hearts became dark and filled with pride. God fashioned us and the earth in a way that pride would eventually die. When we realize that judgment is a bottomless pit of judging and then becoming what we judge, we become aware that our nature of judging causes the same judgment to come upon us and/or our genealogy. Scripture tells us that our sin—*missing the mark* (to mark is to judge)—is passed down to the third and fourth generation. By the revelation of the Holy Spirit, we see and understand that judgment is part of our fallen nature. As we see the effects it has on us from generation to generation, it breaks our hearts and humbles us. I am reminded of the Scripture in Isaiah: "When the Lord shall have washed away the filth of the daughters of Zion, and shall have purged the blood of Jerusalem from the midst thereof *by the spirit of judgment, and by the spirit of burning*" (Isaiah 4:4 KJV, emphasis mine). This burning is painful and produces the fear of the Lord that causes us to cry out for mercy. As God was teaching me these mysteries it was made clear the revelation of the gifts that were brought to Jesus at His birth. Myrrh, frankincense, and gold would reveal the pathway of suffering and bitter weeping, the painful trials that would release the scent of truth and the purity that these two would produce in the human heart. Here I am reminded of the text: "My brethren, count it all joy when ye fall into divers temptations; Knowing this, that the trying of your faith worketh patience. But let patience have her perfect work, that ye may be perfect and entire, wanting nothing" (James 1:2–4 KJV). Without bitter weeping we cannot see. Again we find another hidden truth nestled right with the word as we say—and hear—the word mercy Myrrh-See, we can see that it was there all along. In weeping, we are awakened and are able to see. In my study of chemistry and the human body, I discovered it is the experience of grief and gratitude combined in the presence of the awareness that we are loved by God that produces a chemical reaction enabling the limbic system of the brain to release whatever the body needs to heal. Until I became aware of this truth, healing seemed aloof and mysterious to me. Now, I expect healing and am surprised if and when it does not occur.

God Himself picks up the pieces and removes the stones. He gives us a brand-new heart that can feel again. It feels both pain and pleasure, because it is filled with His Spirit. After this happens we realize the very thing that cursed us, God uses to set us free from our pride and our desire to trust in the knowledge of good and evil. I used to think judgment was bad. On the contrary, **judgments are the fabric used by the Holy Spirit to fashion our garments of humility that deliver us from the pride of life.** God is gracious and full of wisdom, lacking nothing—including a remedy to set us free. Truth that sets us free is strong and does not require any help from us. God is not weak and He is able to do far above that which we as humans could hope or imagine.

When we become aware of our pride, judgments, denial, our trade mentality, and God's love at the same time, we are forever transformed. Our hearts melt like wax. It is this kind of intimate relationship that impels us to love one another. It is not an act of obedience. It is much deeper and not of our logic nor decision-making. On the contrary, it is the very nature of Jesus shining through our dark nature like the light shining out of a lamp that has no light of its own.

This is how walking in love is supposed to take place. It becomes a natural outflow of our union with our husband. Otherwise, it will be a heavy yoke and burden that we will strive to accomplish with only limited success.

When we deal with our own heart issues, our spouse will feel the relief of us backing off. Does this mean that our spouses are off the hook and will never be required to deal with their hearts? What if only one person gets a new heart and then the other remains hard as a stone? Fear not; once your heart is made whole, you will be so in touch with your feelings that allowing another to abuse or disrespect you will not continue. As our hearts heal, we learn to respect ourselves and require it of others. Enabling others to dishonor us becomes a thing of the past. No doormats here.

A Word to Men

Ladies, let me take a moment and speak directly to men. For centuries, women have attempted to change their husbands without success. We can't change ourselves, so I am not sure why we even thought it was possible to change our husbands. Maybe it was our way of avoiding the pain that we held inside. For me, it was my futile attempt to make my husband meet all of my needs. This is so unfair and could never work. Only God is able to meet the needs of mankind. I personally set my husband up for failure and even began to look for it. The pattern we began to follow was—I set up the expectations and he failed to meet them. No wonder he felt like a failure. Who wouldn't? Let me offer, on behalf of all women, a most sincere apology. Since the beginning this has been the pattern that has been passed down from generation to generation. I pray that now is the time for this fruitless merry-go-round to stop. One of the reasons I am writing this book is to get women to go deep inside their own hearts and find God, thereby releasing the men from this cycle of failure where they too can safely enter their hearts and heal. Ladies, I hope you will join me in taking responsibility for your part in the destruction of our marriages. Truly it takes two.

After I realized that my husband was not my god, I tried to be his. This didn't work either. So again, I offer a sincere apology and ask for forgiveness. In the book of Titus, it tells the older women to teach the younger women how to be godly. May this book start a revolution among women to no longer look to our husbands to be our god and to surrender the need to be their god. Let us understand the nature of a woman and find our identity in who God says we are rather than looking to knowledge of good and evil to decide that for us. This requires us to trust God, not man, not even ourselves. We need true heart surrender. When our hearts heal, our reality changes without the need to change someone else.

To heal, we must also let go of our old ways. This will require us to learn a new language, one of the kingdom of the heart. It is a vocabulary developed on purpose in order to express the heart in truth and love. The Bible says that a wise man will study how to communicate, and I hope this book will assist you in that endeavor. Both men and women need to learn how to emotionally communicate. This requires vulnerability and transparency. You can trust this will hurt, and only God will be the one who can heal your broken heart. While we learn to express and listen, we must also seek God to be the one to give us understanding. Take note, the logical brain will be the most difficult part to overcome. It is what we have trusted most of our life. It is time to open the gateway to our heart, and God will not disappoint us. Love will do what we were not able to.

Men are instructed to love their wives, as Christ loves the Church and gave Himself for it. How did He do this? Yes, He did die, but He did so much more. "Seeing then that we have a great high priest, that is passed into the heavens, Jesus the Son of God, let us hold fast our profession. For we have not a high priest which cannot be touched with the *feeling* of our infirmities; but was in all points tempted like as we are, yet without sin" (Hebrews 4:14-15 KJV, emphasis mine). What kind of high priest is Hebrews referring to? "As he saith also in another place, Thou art a priest for ever after the order of

Melchizedek. Who in the days of his flesh, *when he had offered up prayers and supplications **with strong crying and tears** unto him that was able to save him from death, and was heard in that he feared; though he were a Son, yet learned he obedience by the things which he **suffered**;* and being made perfect, he became the author of eternal salvation unto all them that obey him; called of God a high priest after the order of Melchizedek. Of whom we have many things to say, and hard to be uttered, seeing ye are dull of hearing" (Hebrews 5:6-11 KJV, emphasis mine).

Jesus, even though He was the Son of God, suffered after the order of the High Priest Melchizedek. That means He suffered in every form of sorrow and piercing and did not misunderstand any sorrow in order to know our hearts. He declared that if we suffered with Him, we would reign with Him. This is a mystery that reveals how men can love their wives. It is quite simple, but not easy to endure. Basically, it means to feel all emotions, painful and pleasurable. While in them, seek God and allow Him to extract the understanding hidden in them. This is intimacy.

This kind of intimacy is much deeper than words can express. It is this kind of knowing that is the unseen union between two hearts, which produces a bond that surpasses commitment and duty. It is a love that is stronger than death. When people walk in this way, they feel cherished. The fruit that results is passion that refuses to die. It is so amazing that a person will fight to keep it alive and nurture it at all cost. We will guard our hearts, for we will understand that out of them flow all of the issues of life.

Remember in the Hebrew, the word *yada* (to know) means intercourse. It is also the word used where Jesus was "acquainted" with grief. So how is it possible to have *yada* with grief? Note that which is seen is temporary, and everything created reveals the unseen things of God. Well, sex is visible and it is temporary. Emotions are invisible and eternal. Unity in the emotions is the same as a blood covenant. Emotions run through the spiritual heart, and blood runs through the physical heart. When we are in sorrow and suffering, we call that a bleeding heart. Jesus offered us broken bread (His body).

We are the broken body of Christ. Have you ever considered who broke the bread (us, His body)? Jesus broke the bread. No one else came in and took the bread from Jesus and broke it, and no one took His life. He offered the cup, and likened it to His suffering and blood. When He was on the cross and He cried out, "It is finished!"

What does it mean that it was finished? Jesus was actually saying so much more. The word *finished* has various meanings, such as "caput, crown, complete, and bride." The veil of the temple was torn. Just like a virgin who lies with her husband, her veil is torn. This was the marriage consummation spiritually. When the women came to the tomb to anoint the body of Jesus, the angel said to them, "Come, see the place where the Lord lay" (Matthew 28:6 ASV). This word *lay* means to be appointed and comes from a word that means to lie horizontal and to conceive or copulate. The revelation here is that in death He became one with us that we might be one with Him in the resurrection as well. It was, and still is, the marriage blood-covenant union. Therefore, this is how Jesus cherished us and laid down His life. It means to suffer together in bloody copulation. Only then can we reign with Him. Moreover, when a man and woman will suffer with each other emotionally, for the purpose of healing, then we too shall reign together.

Heartfelt intimacy is eternal and that is where our focus needs to be. When heartfelt intimacy is understood and experienced, the physical will portray what the two have already experienced in the heart. This, too, is beyond what the logical mind can experience.

In addition to physical and emotional intimacy (*yada*), here are a few other words that convey *yada*: "respect, honor, understanding, to feel the same feelings, to be in unity, to feel understood, the place where two experience the same emotions or experience." Notice how valuable these are to have a healthy relationship of any kind.

Husbands, can we assume that you want to sexually please your wife? Is it clear yet that your physical capabilities are not all that it will take to please her? If you are not able to cherish her heart yet, that is OK. How can you, if you haven't understood your own? It is the hope of Michael and I that our vulnerability and transparent stories assist you and spark a hunger in you to dig deep and experience your own heart with God first. Take the time to experience your broken heart and let Jesus show you how much He cherishes you. You might think *I am just not like that.* Remember, God made you tender and compassionate just like Him. Take time and find out where you had to become someone else in order to survive the pains in your life.

After that, you will be awakened to your own emotional needs. This will impel you to cherish your wife's needs. It will not be a chore; on the contrary, it will be a spontaneous joy.

Some of you may be wondering why this was not needed in the beginning of the relationship. Remember, women either feel emotionally connected or emotionally dead, and then she tries to get you to be her god. People can't make other people whole. Women don't understand this until their lover fails at it.

That is why you will feel the blame at first. If the marriage doesn't heal, blame will destroy the relationship altogether. Therefore, at first, sex and your love for her will deceive her into thinking that you have made her complete. She will want you to do this over and over. Because of her nature, it will not work. Emotionally deadness will cause people to use sex to feel alive and connected.

Can you see how men and women use each other and their own bodies in order to feel loved? Because a woman's heart is connected to her womb, eventually she will not be able to keep her crying heart silent. Sexual euphoria eventually waxes cold, and the realization that sex alone can't satisfy her wakes up her wounded heart.

Moreover, if at first she did feel emotionally connected and that ceases, she will withdraw and may not even understand why. Remember, using sex, food, drugs, work, religion, shopping, or any other means to take the place of God will eventually hit us in the face, and we will be required to deal with it. Only God can make a heart feel complete. No man can fill God's shoes, and no woman can successfully make her husband her god.

Once a woman finds her identity in God, the husband may initially feel abandoned. Be encouraged—you are not able to make another person's heart whole, so this is a good thing.

In the beginning of my awakening, I became angry and then moved to another extreme. I became very independent. This was not a healthy solution, but it was a necessary process. In leaving my codependent behavior, I needed to understand how unhealthy self-protection manifesting as independence was. It was just as deceptive and destructive to our marriage. Being independent was really an expression of my offense and pride. With this mindset, I attempted to assist God in fixing my husband as if I were his god. As you can image, this too was misery for everyone. Healthy relationship is neither needy nor anti-social. A healthy relationship in God produces a healthy interdependent relationship that works just like Jesus explained—each of us being a unique body part, each supplying one to another in balance yet functioning as one unit.

Only after realizing that neither of us was God, I then turned to God fully, seeking for my identity. This process took quite a bit of time, and Michael and I discussed our issues often. We both saw that our marriage was sick, but neither of us wanted a divorce. We agreed to work on this together. It was like entering a foreign land; neither of us knew the emotional language of the heart, but we were willing to learn.

Often times we felt like we were walking on our tip-toes, hoping we were on the right path. He would say or do something in an attempt to cherish my heart, and later on whisper, "Are we having emotional intimacy?" We would laugh and I would respond by letting him know if my heart felt loved and cared for or not. God was becoming my source, and patience was becoming spontaneous. This could be fun, but there were times when it was frustrating. We both were trusting God to remove our walls of protection that had held us back from true intimacy. In fact, the walls that may have protected us in the past had become walls that were dividing us as a couple. Without God, we could not tear them down.

We were too scared that we would get hurt again. We did hurt each other, but God was faithful to show us the truth about our situation. We both began to understand that our relationship with each other was a mirror image of our relationship with God. However we treated God, and whatever we sowed into our relationship with God, we experienced the mirror effect in our marriage—be it painful or pleasurable

We would talk about what worked and what didn't and then agree on a nonverbal code that we could use in public to let the other person know that we were feeling dishonored or devalued. We did not want to expose our issues in public, yet it was often in public that our behaviors made each other feel hurt and belittled. We did not want to add more pain to our already wounded souls. For example, if he said something critical in front of the extended family, I would wait a minute, then walk over and touch his shoulder and say, "Honey, I am ready to go home; I will see you later."

I would show genuine affection, kiss him goodbye, and leave without letting the rest of the family know that I was hurting. It was never his intent to hurt me, and often he was not even aware of the hurtful language he was using toward me. We were learning how to seek the Kingdom of God that was inside of each other.

By setting such guidelines, we were able to take note of the current situation, remove ourselves from others, and then in private work on whatever the issue was. This protected us and our marriage from any added stress of our family members. Our intent was to find the truth in our problems and then heal. We realized that if one person won any argument, then we both would lose our intimacy. Love and concern for each other and our marriage became our motivation.

Find what works for you. We tried making lists and then reading them instead of speaking them. This allowed us to process rather than defend.

Women, you may want to ask your husband what would make him feel cherished. Michael told me that spending time with him, touch of any kind, and respecting myself and him made him feel cherished.

While working with women, I discovered there are some common things that make a woman feel emotionally cherished. Tender touches when sex is not the motive. Things like holding hands, stroking her hair, being held closely in his arms, having his arm around her shoulder, having his hand around her waist, etc.

I am not saying that these kinds of touches can't lead to sexual intimacy, but if a man touches her this way only to have sexual intercourse, she will feel used and hurt. Remember, it is the heart from which all of these issues flow. Loving-kindness toward the hearts of others, in the same manner in which we are receiving from Christ, is the key. How can we give something to another that we have not yet received from God? We can't.

Looking into each other's eyes when having a conversation will cause one to feel valued and important. Remember, the emotional feelings are paramount in the relationship; this is especially true for the woman. Scripture encourages the man to give the affection due his wife. This is talking about emotional affection. Moreover, when Christ loved the church He suffered every sorrow and suffering for the purpose of knowing our hearts. The objective is to know intimately the heart of your wife, and the actions will match the feelings. She will know it by the way you touch and speak with her.

Looking deep into a woman's eyes is also very powerful and intimate. When words of affection and love are also spoken while looking deep into a woman's eyes, the effects are multiplied.

Back in the day, Michael told me, "I am just not emotional like you are."

I replied, "What if I said to you, 'Sex? Yuck! I am just not sexual like you are.'"

Do you see how crazy that sounds? The truth is men are emotional, and when they allow God in to heal the broken heart they are amazed at how fun life (and sex) can be. Partners with healed, open, fearless hearts make the best lovers.

Let this list of ideas spark your imagination as you grow intimately with your wife. Find out what works for your relationship. Neither men nor women come with rules or steps to follow. Each of us is unique and wonderfully made by God. Maybe that is why women keep the men wondering.

The objective is to learn and heal in our relationship with God as a child and as the bride. God will show us how to affectionately speak to the heart of each other. In so doing, our desire to give our whole hearts will arise and physical bodies can't resist the opportunity to reflect such intimacy.

Take note, men, God made a woman primarily emotional, and if her heart does not feel cherished, something as simple as your touch or the sound of your voice could make her skin crawl. God graced her in this way to keep her from using her body in defilement.

Remember, most women have felt this but, because of fear, have never told their lover. It is time that men know the entire truth so that it can be addressed. If not, the heart will not heal. If our good men, who love their wives, are not afforded the entire truth, how can they be expected to face the issues and resolve the problems? Many good men lose their wives to a would-be player who knows all the right things to say, playing on the emotions of another man's wife with no real intent to love and cherish her.

Angela Bertone

Don't let your wife be the prey of a wolf in sheep's clothing. If she is full and you quench her thirst, she will never drink from a ditch nor eat from a dumpster. Only a starving soul will be driven to such measures.

Chapter 9: What Can Emotions Do for You?

Men and emotions. These two words together may seem foreign at times. We have been conditioned as a society to think that men are supposed to control their feelings. Men have been taught by example and by unspoken rules that emotions are feminine. Therefore, in an attempt to keep their masculinity, men have trained themselves to keep their emotions to a minimum. If you take any love relationship and remove the emotions, you will find a dead relationship. Emotion is what makes us spiritually alive. Emotions are to the spirit what blood is to the body. Our hearts can beat, our lungs can breathe, but if we do not have emotions we will lose our will to live. Unfortunately, this mentality has left many men struggling hopelessly in anger and aggression. In attempting to control their own emotions, they often try to control others. This is not possible. It is an illusion that traps them in cycles they cannot escape. Some are even overtaken by rage, leaving scars upon the hearts of the ones they love. I propose this can stop. Men are the glory of God, and God is Love. Therefore, when a man is restored by the heart of Jesus, it is love that flows. Jesus is the King of the brokenhearted. Let's return to our first love and let our hearts live again.

It does not matter if you are watching a football game packed with intense aggression or sharing a romantic dinner charged with words of affection; both are driven by the life force called emotion.

"And I will sprinkle clean water upon you, and ye shall be clean: from all your filthiness, and from all your idols, will I cleanse you. A new heart also will I give you, and a new spirit will I put within you; and I will take away the stony heart out of your flesh, and I will give you a heart of flesh. And I will put my Spirit within you, and cause you to walk in my statutes, and ye shall keep mine ordinances, and do them. And ye shall dwell in the land that I gave to your fathers; and ye shall be my people, and I will be your God" (Ezekiel 36:25-28 ASV). This text confirms that without a tender, emotional heart filled with God's Spirit, we are not able to walk with God. Still, we will continue to trust in the work of our task-oriented hands and deceive ourselves with the illusion that we can keep the commandments out of our will to do so. This Scripture reveals that the problem and the solution to our condition is hidden inside of the eternal heart.

The law is both eternal and limited. Our flesh is limited, but our spirit is eternal. In order for us to understand eternal and finite, God gave us both the seen and the unseen. He created everything by speaking words. However, without a form we could only hear and not see them. Therefore, God carved and formed all things. This included the law. The law written on our hearts and on stone. Moreover, He created a tree so that we could experience it with sight, smell, taste, touch, and the snake for the whisper. A form of the law exists in letters and words, which produced conclusions in our thought calculations. The tree was given to reveal the full understanding of law. It was in a tangible form placed in the earth, to show the nature of the letter of the law versus the spirit of the law, which would only be understood after their intimacy was broken. God is all-knowing and is in all places at all times. However, only God is powerful enough to handle all knowledge. God is so loving that He would not withhold His heart from us, and inside of His heart exists all knowledge. The nature of this created form was to allow God's children to see that judgment existed both in the earth and in heaven—the seen and the unseen. This was done by God making the roots of the tree hidden in the soil and the canopy of the tree open in the air. Moreover, it showed that it would produce after its own kind eternally. Human nature would soon comprehend this understanding of God's nature firsthand. They would in time do so by the act of seeing its fruit, hearing its whisper, touching its form, smelling its aroma, tasting its fruit, and experiencing the curse of it. Remember, it was given in love and by love, which is eternal. In the word curse is the meaning to cut or split in order to see or understand. God knew that in time and at the appointed time, man would awaken by the Spirit of God and return to God with the desire for relationship based on intimacy and love and not by a set of rules of right and wrong.

Its origin is spiritual like God. We can say, therefore, the law is "**in**" the spirit of love, which is eternal, while at the same time is limited when rooted in the earth or soil; and soil is part of the nature of the human. It is by the act of humans taking hold of what only God can do that we experience the pain of trying to walk in God's shoes. Only then do we return to God broken, humble, and seeking grace and mercy, which is the desire of God's heart. He eagerly awaits the return of each and every person.

When we try to apply the law out of our limited experiences—our human (fleshly) understanding and our actions—it causes sin, which dwells in us, to have power over us and we can't keep the law entirely. Sin is missing the mark or calculation. The definition of the word *mark* is a unit of weight and it comes from the Hebrew word *oth*. One of its meanings is to calculate. Because we can only see in part, our judgments are formed by our limited perception. We may keep God's law in part, but just the thought of murder or adultery deems us guilty of the same. When we attempt to obey the law, we are forced to judge everything through the knowledge of good and evil. This act of judgment requires, by the same law, that we have understanding of the situations that we judge. Thereby, we are now damned to experience the same measure of judgment upon our own lives and in the lives of our children. This is seen through the third and fourth generations and becomes an endless cycle. This cycle is an abyss of sorrow and suffering, pain and grief, all brought on by our attempts at judging. Jesus warned that whatever we judge, we will be judged with the same measure of judgment. I use the phrase "judge and become" as a short phrase to remind us of Matthew chapter seven. Let's awaken to the fact that we are stuck, or nailed, to the judging and becoming tree. This is why only God is able to handle the authority and power that is held within the requirements of the law. Humans are too weak because our flesh can only handle limited power. Judgment is an eternal power that only love can wield.

In Romans, it talks about the flesh and the mind. Please note, when it speaks of the flesh it means "when taken unto oneself, to prefer oneself, to drag, to be carnally minded." When it speaks of the mind, it is the word *nous* and it comes from the word *ginosko*.

These are Greek words that can also be understood by studying the intimate Hebrew word *yada*. This is that word we spoke of earlier, "to know." It does not just include the mind but the feelings in our heart, the desires in our heart, and the thoughts of the mind. The mind will calculate through the five senses in the flesh and the spiritual five senses in the emotions. Our opinions, feelings, and desires together calculate, conclude, and agree or disagree through the limbic brain that we spoke of earlier. Remember, the frontal lobe is where task and reward or punishment impulses are. This is the carnal mind. Risk verses reward is in the carnal mind alone. The emotions are in the heart-brain and in the limbic brain. Remember, emotional memories are held in the limbic, and when they are formed from a belief of not being loved they will need to heal. This is why God fills our hearts with His Spirit. Even if we believe one hundred percent in our frontal lobe that we are loved by God, if we feel forsaken in our hearts we will produce cycles of rejection. That is why the task-oriented, risk verses reward decisions will not produce lasting intimacy in our relationship with God or anyone else. The law that is held in our frontal lobe must die for the spirit of the law to arise in our hearts. When we use our logic to conclude a matter like "I am loved by God because the Word of God says so," yet we feel forsaken, the logical brain will actually cause us to fight harder to feel loved. We will use the law and rules to try and get better and obey more to feel loved. This will also lead to justification, minimization, and rationalization rather than godly sorrow that leads us unto repentance. This is why the law kills relationship. It is the spirit that gives life. The mystery of the spirit of the law is death. Death to relationship built on rules. Yet this death has no sting. On the contrary, it births newness of life in Christ our husband. That is why the letter kills, but the spirit gives life. Both are a form of death. The spirit being a death in order to resurrect unity and intimacy and the letter being the death unto condemnation, which will only produce the need to *do* more to earn acceptance. It is time for this mentality that trades goodness for love to die.

If my husband is with me because he made a vow and not because he is drawn to me with love and passion, what do we have? We have a relationship of the logical law and a written commitment. The law is good, but God wants us to live by the spirit of the law. This is not so that we can do away with the law, but to rather to walk in love, which is what the entire law is established in.

This is the basic difference between a written covenant on paper with pen and a spiritual covenant written on our hearts with the finger of God. A man can hire a maid, a babysitter, a cook, and a prositute. However, a wife is never for hire. God said he would not take a bribe. As a wife, now I understand why God will not take a bribe.

If I am forced to love my husband because it is my commitment, then we both are missing out on the fullness of the marriage. I am not against commitment. It is part of what has pushed me into the deeper truths of relationship. But make no mistake, it was not commitment alone. It was the drive in me through my emotions to never let the feelings of love die. I was hungry to keep the passion alive, and it was that hunger that kept me when my commitment was weak. Remember, if we could speak with the tongues of angels, unveil all mysteries, and give our bodies to be burned but did not have love, then we are just a clanging brass. It would all be vanity. If love is a duty, someone please give me a toilet. If love is only a commitment, then someone please commit me.

Consider the fruit of the Spirit. Fruit is produced on the branch of a tree or vine. The branch does not *do* anything to make the fruit. As long as the branch abides on the vine and is nourished by it, receiving warmth, water, nutrients, and fertilization, over time the fruit develops. In actuality, by itself the branch is helpless.

Our bodies prefer limits, rules, and boundaries. This is the nature of matter. However, spirit, light, wind, and water do not have boundaries. God breathed into us His nature, which is not bound or measurable by humans. Love and all the fruits of the Spirit are not measurable, and against such there is no law or limits. Spirit is like the mist—a mixture of water and air. It carries in its nature all possibilities.

Our borders of flesh have a nature of limits or slavery. From the moment mankind trusted in the knowledge that came from outside of our relationship with God, we died and became bound by knowledge. In so doing, we became slaves to knowledge and rules. Adam, one man, passed this nature to all mankind in his seed. Death and slavery became our condition from which Jesus would set us free. The apostle Paul expressed this same frustration in the book of Romans.

"For we know that the *law is spiritual*: but I am carnal, sold under sin. For that which I do I know not: for not what I would, that do I practise; but what I hate, that I do. But if what I would not, that I do, I consent unto the law that it is good. So now it is no more I that do it, but sin which dwelleth in me. For I know that in me, that is, in my flesh, dwelleth no good thing: for to will is present with me, but to do that which is good is not. For the good which I would I do not: but the evil which I would not, that I practise. But if what I would not, that I do, it is no more I that do it, but sin which dwelleth in me. I find then the law, that, to me who would do good, evil is present. For I delight in the law of God after the inward man: but I see a different law in my members, warring against the law of my mind, and bringing me into captivity under the law of sin which is in my members. Wretched man that I am! who shall deliver me out of the body of this death? I thank God through Jesus Christ our Lord. So then I of myself with the *mind*, indeed, serve the law of God; but with the *flesh* the law of sin" (Romans 7:14-25 ASV, emphasis mine).

As Christians, we trust in the Word that tells us we who are in Christ now have the power to become the sons of God—Jesus, being the first born of many. When our identity is settled in sonship, then we are no longer slaves. What would be our evidence of this taking place in our lives? We would no longer fulfill the lust of our flesh. The primary lust of the flesh is to avoid pain and embrace pleasure.

Ezekiel 36 is the promise that we *shall* walk in His statutes and keep His commandments. Moreover, Jesus said the ones who keep the will of the Father are the ones who love Him. In addition, He told us that if we cannot love the ones we can see, how can we love God whom we cannot see? Then to top it off, He told us that if we don't forgive, then we will not be forgiven.

In close relationships people hurt people, especially in a marriage. I found it difficult to continue forgiving the same offenses over and over. In my mind, if someone was truly sorry for an offense and they continued to do the same thing over and over, then the apology didn't seem real. I could not figure out how to forgive seventy times seven. On the contrary, I would find my heart waxing cold. This was not only true in my marriage but with my parents, siblings, friends, or anyone who was stuck in a pattern of treating me with dishonor. These problems, coupled with the words of Jesus, stirred in me and my heart became troubled. I knew there were people who, no matter how much I tried to forgive by an act of my will or decision in my mind, I still found myself bound to with unforgiveness in my heart. No matter how hard I tried to keep the commandments and to love, I continually fell short. Did this mean that I was not a son of God? What does the Bible say? "If a man say, I love God, and hateth his brother, he is a liar: for he that loveth not his brother whom he hath seen, how can he love God whom he hath not seen? And this commandment have we from him, That he who loveth God love his brother also" (1 John 4:20-21 KJV). Just before this Scripture we are informed that the only way we can love Him is because He first loved us. However, knowing this in our frontal lobe while feeling forsaken in our hearts will leave us a prisoner of unforgiveness, trapped by the shackles of judgment. This is the condition of our broken hearts, and unforgiveness is the evidence that testifies against us, forcing us to stay in the prison until we pay the debt in full.

This only happens when we see our judgment and are filled with humility and cry out for mercy. When He bestows His mercies upon us, then a supernatural, spontaneous flood of forgiveness busts out of us. For me, often I was judging Michael and trying to forgive him. Only God set me free from this abyss.

At this point in my life I began to see what hindered me from living the life that Jesus said a believer would live. I saw from Scripture, as a fallen man, I had at least three major problems—I judged others using the knowledge of good and evil; I would hide and run from the truth and, therefore, God; and I would blame and defend myself from others. In short, I would accuse, run, or fight.

This is an uncontrollable act—something I did even when I tried not to. I would justify my judging by the Word to try to ease my guilt. Finally, the Lord showed me that I am a judge according to Genesis. After Adam and Eve ate and became like gods, knowing both the knowledge of good and evil, God put them out of the garden to protect them from eating from the Tree of Life and living eternally in that fallen condition. Matthew 7 brings revelation to this condition and tells us that however we judge, we will be judged in the same manner. He then comforted us by telling us He did not come to condemn us but rather to give us abundant life. We must understand this part of our nature and face it with open eyes and an open heart. God is the only one who can use this situation for our good to transform us. In fact, as I mentioned before, it is our judgments that condemn us, and it is by the same judgment that God delivers us from our pride.

We desire to hide and cover our shame, but to push it down into our hearts is a fruitless effort. It is amazing that we actually think we are able to hide anything from God! Shame and guilt are emotions that are given to us as indicators. Denying our emotions and attempting to escape them is part of our nature to self-protect. Confession is with the mouth, and the feelings of godly sorrow are felt with the heart.

Ephesians 4 tells us that when we go past our emotions, we are then given over to all manner of lasciviousness, which means wantonness and vanity. To sum it up, when we push our emotions down, it will cause us to do all manner of evil. We blame and find fault. Rather than seeking understanding in our hearts and in the hearts of others, we look to our past experiences and trust they will deliver us.

When I became aware of my judgments, I realized that I was actually doing all the things I had judged others for—especially my husband. I fell on my face and cried out for help. I realized as long as I simply judged right from wrong, I was setting myself up for the same sin. Oh, it may have not been the same exact act, and the details may have been different, but the actual judgment was the same. For example, I judged my husband for watching too much football and not spending enough time with me. Though this judgment may have been accurate, God did not create me as a judge. In my whining to God, He showed me I treated Him (God) the same way. Even though I did not watch any football, I still did the same by not spending much time with God, whom I said I loved.

So, what is the answer? If we seek the Kingdom, then all these things shall be added to us. It is clear in the Scriptures that Jesus seeks the hearts of men, knows what the mind of the Holy Spirit is, makes intercession, and prays the will of God. Learning these principles changed my life. It is so simple, yet hidden in plain sight. Let's look at how seeking the heart can free us from judgment and being damned to becoming the same as what we judged, as Jesus warned in Matthew 7.

When the Lord spoke to me and revealed I was doing the same things I had judged others for, I was filled with great grief. My shame was evident and my heart was broken. I no longer looked at my husband as right or wrong, but rather I began to seek to know his heart and ask God to help me understand what was happening on the inside of him. When I became aware of the times I had acted the same way, instant forgiveness would flow from my heart in humility toward my husband. It became impossible to hold unforgiveness toward my husband, as God was revealing my own sin that I was now needing grace for.

When I would admit that I was not different and that if I were in his shoes I would do the same, it caused me to intercede for him and seek God for wisdom to respond in each and every situation. I often cried for mercy for the both of us. I needed mercy, because I had judged and was now open to becoming that same thing by the curse of the law. However, in humility and fear of the Lord, I cried out for grace and mercy. I now understand how God gives grace to the humble. Becoming all that you judge will humble you pretty quick. Once I saw that I was everything that I judge, there was a strong reverence birthed inside my soul. This revelation causes us to not esteem ourselves higher than another. I actually became impelled to pray for mercy and wait for direction. I would feel my pain, seek to feel His heart, and stay out of my logic. I would wait for God and He would bring about the perfect situation for Michael and me to work things out.

God was teaching me to stay focused on the heart. Seeking each other's hearts will produce understanding, and that brings us into intimacy.

Judgments are a natural part of our everyday lives, and they are usually accurate. However, the laws associated with judgment require the one doing the judging to actually partake in the same. Once awakened to this law, we become humble and no longer desire to trust in the knowledge of good and evil. Moses told the people in Deuteronomy 1:39 that only those who did not trust in the knowledge of good and evil would enter into the Promised Land. This is still true for us today. So, rather than trusting in knowledge of good and evil, we seek the heart for understanding. In the book of Proverbs, we are encouraged to seek understanding, even if it costs us all we have. Solomon prayed for an understanding heart, and God was so moved by this prayer, He gave him wisdom above all others. So, understanding is a principal thing.

The Eve/female part of every human is our emotional part, where we experience intimacy of the heart. Emotions are the pathway to understanding. "Counsel in the heart of man is like deep water; but a man of understanding will draw it out" (Proverbs 25:5 ASV). Our nature is to push emotions down, but God instructs us to draw them out and not disregard them. We are instructed to trust God with all our hearts and to not lean on our own understanding. That means don't trust our logic, opinions, or judgments about the emotions. When we trust God with them, He shall direct our path. It is very difficult to do this, because it is the opposite of our nature. The emotions are the senses of the spirit. The mystery of iniquity is the fact that in pride our judgments cause us to esteem one person above another. Moreover, in our attempt to push painful emotions away we judge the person and our emotions as bad or negative. This will then cause us to go past our feelings in an attempt to avoid reacting to the painful event. It is at this point that we are now given over to all manner of lasciviousness. This is where we missed the mark and the opportunity to lift up the pain to God for help in our time of need. Unless we exercise our emotional senses and mature, by lifting them up to God for Him to redeem them as we learn to lean not unto our own understanding of them, we are held prisoner to our own judgments. Hebrews 5 tells us to exercise these senses so that we can mature and eat strong meat. This was not speaking of the five natural senses of sight, smell, taste, touch, and hearing. If so, we would all be able to eat of this meat that Paul spoke of on numerous occasions.

Jesus gave us some clues as to where the spiritual senses are. "And Jesus perceiving it saith unto them, Why reason ye, because ye have no bread? do ye not yet perceive, neither understand? have ye your heart hardened?" (Mark 8:17 ASV). "For this people's heart is waxed gross, and their ears are dull of hearing, and their eyes they have closed; lest haply they should perceive with their eyes, and hear with their ears, and understand with their heart, and should turn again, and I should heal them" (Matthew 13:15 ASV). It is clear that our spiritual senses are in the heart; therefore, they are in the emotions.

It is vital for all of us to allow God to break through the deadness of our hearts. The time is now to ask God to remove the calluses that we have constructed in our futile efforts of self-protection. All the pains of our past have assisted us in forging a wall built from our past perceptions. This is the same as the wall of Jericho. *Jericho* comes from the Hebrew word *ruach*, which means fragrance, and fragrance means to perceive. Therefore, Jericho actually means perception. Note, the children of Israel were forbidden to take anything from that battle. This wall was as thick as it was tall and only God could destroy it. This is a type and shadow of the walls we have all built around our hearts. Remember, the word "serpent" in the book of Genesis actually means learned experiences. This is knowledge of right and wrong that we have used to build up this wall. Now, are we willing to let go of trusting in this knowledge so that we can enter into the promises of God?

Unless we are broken and surrender our self-protection, we will not be able to receive the Spirit of understanding. There are seven Spirits of God and they are here to bring us into all truth by way of the Holy Spirit. This is communicated through the healed emotions. Jesus is the King of the brokenhearted, and He is here to heal our emotions so that He can rule in them.

It had become obvious that I had run from my own heart and had spent a lifetime trying to escape my painful emotions. God was going deep into my heart and using my pain to show me His heart and all that grieved Him. Moreover, it was only through pain that I was beginning to understand the hearts of others, especially my husband. In fact, the reality that we face in our broken marriages shows us that we are not healed. It is when we awaken to God's love toward us that His love then flows through us. In that union, we love others as we are loved.

It is this kind of love that takes my breath away and buckles my knees. Only after I experienced this with Jesus did I begin to experience it in my marriage. Jesus is the real thing, and Michael is the image of God.

It finally became evident how the human natural marriage relationship is a gift to help us enter into physical intimacy so that we can understand spiritual intimacy. Unless we allow God to do this for us, we will not experience it. The Scriptures teach us that a true Jew is one who has circumcised his heart, not his flesh. Moreover, it tells us that the Word of God comes first to the Jew and then to the Gentile. So, it is imperative that we allow Jesus to circumcise our hearts and heal our broken emotions. Without this process, we will not be able to experience true intimacy at its deepest level with God, nor with others.

Let me put it bluntly here. If a woman does not feel an emotional intimacy with her spouse, it is evident that the spouse is not giving his wife what she needs to be fulfilled in the relationship. This is also evidence of his relationship with God. I am not saying that the man doesn't love God and is not intimate at all. I am saying the man is not living as the bride of Christ. Rather, he is living as a child of God, and a child and slave are treated the same. "But I say that so long as the heir is a child, he differeth nothing from a bondservant though he is lord of all; but is under guardians and stewards until the day appointed of the father" (Galatians 4:1-2 ASV). Emotions are the most important part of a woman's sexuality. The good news is that emotional maturity and unity really is not that difficult once the heart is healed and is no longer in self-protect mode. Emotional intimacy actually becomes spontaneous. This is the key to spontaneous, exciting, and passionate lovemaking.

The Holy Spirit is our teacher and will teach us all things. Ask God to use the pain of your past to awaken your heart, and begin dealing with any of the old past hurts that you are still protecting yourself from. This is not a fast process, nor is it easy. However, it is most definitely worth it. God is faithful, merciful, and patient. He will take His time with us and the journey will become our joy. Living in the present moment is the desired destination. In so doing, we no longer live from our past, nor do we miss out on our present by worrying about our future.

When we are emotionally healed, and have exercised them, we are able to remain content as Paul explained in this scripture: "I know both how to be abased, and I know how to abound: every where and in all things I am instructed both to be full and to be hungry, both to abound and to suffer need" (Philippians 4:12 KJV; emphasis mine). The marriage union is a beautiful creation of God that He will use to bring up the old that has been buried deep inside. God will use our memories to transform us. In these times, seek your own heart, the heart of your spouse, and the heart of God.

I found, in so doing, that my marriage was actually a mirror image I needed in order to see my relationship with God. This was crushing at first, but it soon revealed God's immeasurable love toward me. As a result, that same kind of love began to flow from me without conscious decision. It was the fruit born out of the intimate way God loved me when I was not lovable according to my own standards.

Jesus said we must be willing to die if we want to truly live. I have discovered that to be true. I had to die to my own way of seeing, my opinions, my judgments, my perceptions, and my self-protection. Only then did I begin to experience the love of God that became tangible and began to flow from my heart while I stood in amazement. I became fully aware it was not me but Christ in me causing such fruit to appear in my life and in my relationship with my husband. In fact, it often surprised Michael and me.

We can only enter the kingdom like a child. But a child can still hide behind walls. Are you ready to enter and be free from all the protections of the past? Are you ready for truth and intimacy that is spontaneous and not laborious? Are you hungry for passion with God and your spouse?

Just as Abraham offered Isaac, we must put our inner child on the altar and trust God can deliver us. He has already provided the ram, which means "rolled together in one." The ram is a picture of Christ and His bride rolled together in unity as one. You will feel like you are going to die. The old nature will struggle to keep you in your logic, and there may be times when you wish you could turn back the clock and retreat behind the wall. However, once you have tasted the spontaneous love of God emotionally with the fullness of your heart, you shall never thirst again for another person, event, or thing to fulfill your heart. Even if you try to return, you will find it impossible. Christ living inside of you becomes so tangible and real that you are impelled to be with Him in all things at all times. You become transformed from an obedient child to a lovesick bride.

Jesus came in the form of flesh that He might experience every sorrow and suffering and not sin. That means that He did not miss the mark—the understanding or calculation—of one of His sorrows or sufferings. Like we discussed before, calculation means understanding. So, you see, He came to understand us intimately in the flesh and in the heart. Are you willing to meet Him in all the places where He is waiting for you? Will you meet Him in rejection, abandonment, false accusation, or betrayal? It is only by suffering with Him that we shall reign with Him. The kingdom is in our hearts. Will you go like a child, vulnerable, unable to defend yourself?

This is how He expressed His mercy—that He would only judge the world after He first had suffered in every manner and experience every temptation that He would one day judge. He understood Matthew 7 and knew that no one is exempt from becoming what one judges, not even Himself. That is why He suffered the judgment just as the law required. If He could not escape, and we are no greater than our master, then we too shall not escape. He was showing us through His suffering. He suffered to know us and died to redeem us. It is by the spirit of judgment that we are humbled and we awaken. This causes us to turn to God with godly sorrow, and this kind of suffering is the pathway to healing our limbic brain and our heart-brain. This is the healing of our subconscious where all of the issues of life flow from. That is why Jesus said if you abide in Me, you shall not sin. Hosea 2:19 says He betrothed us in judgment.

Now, will you go deep into your memories and sorrows for the purpose of knowing what He felt? Just for the sheer purpose of knowing Him? He did that for us. Greater love hath no man than to lay down his life. Will you now lay down your life as the bride of Christ to know Him? This is the mystery of marriage.

Chapter 10: The Affection Due Him

"A worthy woman who can find? for her price is far above rubies" (Proverbs 31:10 ASV).

"For a man indeed ought not to have his head veiled, forasmuch as he is the image and glory of God; but the woman is the glory of the man" (1 Corinthians 11:7 ASV).

"A worthy woman is the crown of her husband; but she that maketh ashamed is as rottenness in his bones" (Proverbs 12:4 ASV).

hat does a man look for in a wife?

- A woman of integrity, honor, and honesty…
- An industrious woman, intelligent and diligent…
- A woman wise, full of understanding…
- A woman with a humble and meek heart…
- A woman of strength, courage, and determination…
- A woman who is dedicated to her family's life…
- A woman who is able to care for and nurture her children…
- A woman of beauty, elegance, and respect…
- A woman of passion, romance, and intimacy…

Is Christ worthy of this kind of wife? Of course He is. This is not the kind of wife I was to my earthly husband, nor to Christ, but it was my desire, and at times I could fulfill some of these attributes. However, in my attempts I would become tired and weary. Where was this abundant life with rest for the weary that I had heard so much about?

No Longer Dis-Eve'd

For years I served God out of a heart of duty, gratitude, commitment, and presumed love. I was hungry for true intimacy but failed to find it.

I worked hard to show my gratitude and prove my love. What? I "worked" very hard to do that? I began to notice my own thoughts and how messed up they were. In my despair, I wondered, *What is intimacy with God and how could I find it?*

My works and illusions were filled with good intentions and what appeared to be a pure heart. I did everything I knew to be a "good Christian." I read my Bible, went to church, prayed, worshiped, tithed, gave alms, and did good deeds; I was careful to avoid even the appearance of evil. I based my judgments on the Bible and what my parents and leaders had taught me. This was my pathway to find righteousness and holiness. It was what everyone was doing. Surly this was the way, right?

I endeavored to be loving, peaceful, patient, kind, gentle, meek, good, faithful, and long suffering, all the while maintaining self-control. The Bible calls these fruits. I was not aware that spiritual fruit could not be a work of my decisions. In fact, to attempt to do an act of kindness out of my ability to decide doesn't make any sense. These are called fruit of the spirit in the Bible, and I was trying to make them happen like they were a rule to follow. God showed me that I was trying to carve a piece of spiritual fruit and that was the same as the work of my hands or idolatry. Fruit is a spontaneous result of intimacy not an act of obedience. Fruit could not be carved by my intentions, decisions, or choices. Fruit is the result of intimacy or abiding in the vine. In my logic, I was convinced that I could do these things as an act of my will. But one major problem confronted me continually—my actions testified against me. And what's worse, carved fruit is not edible. On the contrary, it is only for show, to adorn a table. When we bow down to the work of our own self-righteousness, it is a form of idol worship. Are you carving the fruit of the spirit like I was?

God wants us to be connected and intimate, not good. My attempts at good works were really a hidden form of idolatry, but I was too blind to notice. The knowledge tree had me blind and in an endless pit of judgment and blame. Blame and accusations are the same thing. It didn't take long for me to see who the accuser was and awaken to how intimate I had become with accusations.

I began to go deep into my heart and see the illusions that I was trusting in. In my blindness, I complained often to God about my husband's faults. I fussed about how he did all the right actions, but he did not *know* my heart. I complained that he was not intimate with me emotionally. God very gently said, "I know exactly how you feel. That is how you treat Me." Ugh! This was devastating and sobering to say the least.

I was living my relationship with God out of my knowledge of good and evil, but I wanted my relationship with my spouse to be one of the heart—a union filled with intimacy. What hypocrisy and denial!

Remember that words and seeds are the same thing? When we receive the words of lies based on the knowledge of good and evil, we are not receiving truth. If we are not receiving truth from God, then where did we acquire the lies? Genesis tells us they are from Satan or the serpent. This, again, means our learned experiences. If Christ, who is truth, is my husband, and I am not holding truth in my heart, then how did the lies get there? I became filled with lies by trusting in my past experiences. This is what it means to trust in the knowledge of good and evil rather than trusting in the One who created and formed good and evil. This is what it means to be an adulterer against God.

How could I find rest in God and truly believe that I was loved and cared for? Now that I was aware that I was the spiritual harlot who had become one with lies, I was undone with shame and guilt. I prayed for God to deliver me of these things and even found myself begging, but not resting. I could quote all the Scriptures and do all the spiritual warfare and decree and declare. I even cast down vain imaginations daily, but I could not really find lasting rest. Over and over I would cry, "Where is the life abundant, full of joy?" This must have been what Jesus meant when He called the doubting people an adulterous generation. My life had become a burden of slavery with the task of daily managing my broken emotions. The abundant life was actually not possible through my decision-making. I had been choosing it for years, with very few results. There had to be an answer, but how could I find the way with my blind eyes?

The pain in my life was now beyond measure. The truth about my own soul was crushing the life out of me. This did not seem like a good thing at first, but I can attest now that it was exactly what I needed to wake me up and make me sober-minded. It was at this time that I began to see my judgments and I realized that I had become everything that I had ever judged another to be. Time and time again, it became evident that **I was treating God the same way my husband was treating me. I was, in fact, reaping what I was sowing.** Blame was no longer something that I could find relief in. On the contrary, it had become my mirror. At times, I would walk away by the grace and mercy of God, only to forget what manner of human I was and again create the same mirror image. At first it felt like a curse or trap. However, in time I realized it was the grace and mercy of God for Him to show me, yet again, my twisted ways. God created the world so that everything is from Him and for Him and returns back to Him. He truly is a good, good Father.

Daily I began to see where I had placed the burden of God on my husband's shoulders. By making him my god, I had placed him in an impossible situation. He felt like an utter failure. No man can carry the weight of being a god. He needed a wife who understood him and honored him for who he truly was—a son of God. He was made in the image of God and was to reveal the glory of God, not to be my god.

Looking back, I wonder how he endured. Only after I was able to see my own heart, hurts, and codependency was I able to let go of trying to change him. God told me that to change a cake, only one ingredient needed to change; and He was changing me. At first, I was extremely angry at God and complained about being a doormat. I was starting to understand that no one could love and honor me until I loved and honored me. That left me with another problem. I didn't feel lovable. Moreover, seeing my spiritual adultery and blaming my flesh caused me to lose hope that I could ever rise out of such a pit. After all, humans live in fear and doubt every now and then, right? It didn't seem possible that love could cast out *all* fear. Some, of course, but "all"? This meant I would remain a harlot? How could God love me now? The good news was, and still is, that love is not earnable, for God is love. Man cannot earn God. I wondered, *How deep could this illusion be?*

In time, and through many heartbreaking moments recalled in the recesses of my memory, God revealed His love for me. I not only knew in my logic that God loved me, but I discovered deep in my heartfelt emotions that God loves me and is ever present with me in all things and at all times. It was in this discovery that I became whole. I saw God, and I saw that He alone is love.

I realized why He refused to leave me in delusion, because for God to allow me to believe that I could trade Him for love would be for Him to agree to me being stuck in a harlot mentality. What loving father could allow His child to be a harlot and consent to that way of life? If we, who are evil, can give good gifts to our children, what makes us think that God would do anything less for His? Would you prostitute your child to yourself? Disgusting, right? Here was the evidence that I had judged God and truly did not know Him. However, in His great love and mercy, as I cried out for help He heard me and healed my broken soul. Only then did I discover that I no longer needed to trade with my husband to make me feel whole. I no longer needed him to do a long list of things to make me feel loved. When the truth of love exploded in my heart, I discovered that I was already whole; I was already loved. I no longer wanted to trade with God, nor my husband, nor anyone else for love or approval. As long as I was using my calculations (marks) of my past learned experiences (serpent), I was trading being good in order to receive love. This prostitute mentality no longer had me in a pit of deception. I was free from the trade mentality and my need to fight or run and hide. The wild-beast mentality that we call "fight or flight" could not hold me as its slave any longer. This was the beginning of a whole new way of seeing life and living it. I became free from calculating like an animal whether to run or fight in order to survive. The revelation of God's love through His Son, Jesus, set me free from using judgments to feel love, for now that I was without blame, the trade harlot mentality was no more. I was free from that abyss. I had crossed the Jordan and entered into the land of promises. It was here that the fruit of God was bigger than my head, for the fruit of God is eternal and without measurement and cannot be understood by the carnal mind. Moreover, this land is fat with the milk and honey of God. In fact, it flows like rivers. No need to milk the cow or rob the honeybees. I discovered this land was in my heart and is eternal.

This became the pathway to Michael and me sharing our lives as two whole people, realizing that we were lacking nothing. It was in this kind of intimacy with God that I became the wife my husband was looking for. He was free to be himself. I no longer needed him to fulfill me. Rather, we began to share our sorrows and joys. This was the abundant life that we had heard about and read about but could not find anywhere. It was in waking up to who I am as a woman, created by God for His dwelling place, that I discovered love and healing—nothing missing and nothing broken. Truly, His Word is true and never returns void.

I no longer struggled with needing acceptance or avoiding rejection. I no longer saw division as a problem; rather, I saw every division as a means of multiplication. This produces great expectancy with abundant joy rather than the fear of lack.

As I discovered that in the Kingdom there is no such thing as lack, my mouth began to speak from a place of already being loved rather than trying to get my husband to prove his love. In times past, I would say things like, "If you loved me, you would not treat me that way." That changed spontaneously and I would ask God, "How should I speak to my husband? Please put Your words in my mouth." The beauty of this prayer is that God was and is always faithful to give me the words in the very hour. This keeps me from even needing to figure it out. I am free from calculations. By the way, just in case I didn't mention it before, the word *calculations* is the same word as *mark*. I was free from the mark or calculations of the beast mentality. Freedom is what we have when we see the love of God in Jesus. To miss the mark is so much bigger than I had ever been taught. "Jesus said unto them, If ye were blind, ye should have no sin: but now ye say, We see; therefore your sin remaineth" (John 9:41 KJV). To see here is to have the ability to judge, to perceive, to understand, to calculate the mark, the signal, the flag, the wonder, the beacon, the monument, the omen, the prodigy, the evidence, the sign, the token, the miracle. After studying each of these words, I understand why Jesus called us blind. Without the Holy Spirit to reveal the truth to us, we are not able to see and comprehend. Only in seeing ourselves and others through the eyes of Jesus can we abide in love.

On one occasion, my husband came home from work and he was very snippy with his words. I sat quietly at dinner asking God for understanding of Michael's heart. This is what I do now rather than criticizing him for his speech. I could see he had a rough day at work and was processing and venting from some internal frustrations. The sharp words continued the following evening. I again asked God how to respond.

God spoke to me, "Tell him that you know that he loves you and that he loves you well."

That was all that He gave me.

So I asked Him, "When do I say this, Father?"

He replied, "I will show you."

I walked into the kitchen just as Michael turned the corner, and we were face to face. I felt God move in my emotions with compassion toward us both.

I placed my hands on his cheeks and looked him in his eyes and said, "I know you love me, and you love me well," just like I heard Father say.

I could see the pain in his eyes melt.

I continued, "I am not sure what you are going through, but I want you to know that I am here for you, whether you need to be alone or if you want to talk. And if I have done anything to hurt you, I had no intention of doing so, but I would like to apologize if I hurt you in any way."

With soft words of surprise, he asked me, "Was I mean? Or did I say something?"

"Yes," I said. We talked softly in each other's arms. He had been dishonored at work and was hurting. Moreover, he was not even aware of how he was speaking to me. If I had not already known that I was and am loved by God, I would have needed to defend myself. Moreover, I would have needed to be reassured of Michael's love for me.

However, because my wholeness is in my relationship with God, I did not need to defend myself at all.

What a joy to be a woman who can support her husband in good times and in the painful ones without the burden of grasping for love and acceptance. My old mindsets robbed me of being a woman of honor and integrity, wisdom and understanding. It was only in feeling whole in God and being intimate with God that I was, and am, able to be intimate with my husband. It is from this way of living that the fruits of intimacy are spontaneous and abundant in our everyday life.

Let me encourage you. If you want to be in the place where love and kindness flows freely, then go deep into your own heart first and face the places in your life where you did not feel loved by others. By the time we are seven years old, we have developed a heart-brain and a subconscious brain that believes it needs to do things to get loved. This illusion supports a belief that we can earn love as well as lose it. But love is not purchasable. Love is a person, not an action. ***When the Person of love lives in us, the fruit of love flows through us***. Everyone has a broken heart and we all need to be healed so that love can flow freely through us.

We are told in the Bible that our words come from the overflow of our hearts and that no one can tame their tongue. Prior to my heart healing, my mouth was pretty polluted.

That showed evidence that I needed a new heart. Gossip, slander, murmuring, complaining, and judgments were just some of the trash coming from my heart and overflowing out of my mouth. I could clean up my speech pretty much, but when the heat was on that was when my true colors became evident. No amount of correcting my words could free my heart from the lies deep within. What is your mouth saying when you are pushed to the limit? I suggest you listen to it, instead of saying you didn't mean it or attempting to correct it. If it overflowed, it is in your heart. Take the time to see how it got there. "Search me, O God, and know my heart: try me, and know my thoughts; and see if there be any wicked way in me, and lead me in the way everlasting" (Psalms 139:23-24 ASV).

Do you remember the story of the children of Israel in the wilderness complaining after Moses led them out of slavery? As a result of their words, the snakes bit them and many died. This is a picture of what I was doing too. After I looked at my words, my judgments, and my complaints, I realized that the problems were inside of me and I didn't like it. This did not mean that my husband didn't have any issues. Just like all of us, he did; however, trying to fix another person is useless. On the other hand, when God healed my heart, the way that my husband treated me began to change. That is because "For as he thinketh within himself, so is he" (Proverbs 23:7 ASV), and "As thou hast believed, so be it done unto thee" (Matthew 8:13 ASV). These scriptures have hidden in them the revelation of the power of our beliefs. Because I now knew deep in my heart, through my emotions and because of my emotions, this belief was now locked in my limbic brain. My life was now testifying that I truly believed that I was and am loved. Goodness and mercy actually chases me down now, just like God promised.

Because we are each other's mirror, I could see myself and seek God for help. In addition, after I no longer needed Michael to make me feel a certain way, his old behaviors no longer fit my new behaviors. This left him feeling pretty helpless. At first, he withdrew and became depressed. I let him know that I loved him and would never leave him. I also told him that he was free to leave me if he wanted. I explained that if he wanted to divorce me that was his decision, but that I wanted to spend my entire life with him. When he withdrew into himself, I no longer had the need to beg him for attention or anything for that matter. He was now free to live his life with or without me. I wanted him, but had no need or desire to control him. I was free and at total peace. I could live my life regardless of his actions. This was not normal for our relationship, and at first Michael wasn't sure my new behavior would last. The good news is, it did last. He wasn't aware, but it was not me doing something. God had healed me and was further healing my heart. My actions were the overflow of the love I felt from God, not from the actions of him or others.

God had taught me the pathway into intimacy through being a wife. I longed for my husband to know my heart, yet I had avoided my own heart my entire life. How could I expect my husband to know my heart if I was not willing to know my own heart? Moreover, how could I know another person's heart if I could not know my own? It was by going deep into my pains and letting God reveal and rewrite my understanding that I became free from all my fears, especially the fear of rejection and loneliness.

The only thing I can liken these experiences to is the conception and birth of my children. Just like a virgin woman submits her body to be broken to receive her husband's seed, so it is with the Lord of our hearts. Jesus breaks our hearts with the truth of our past and then places His words in us. The bloody pain of our past holds in it the power needed for the words of God to grow and produce the fruit of love and compassion. At first when pregnant, we feel a mixture of painful emotions that are confusing and arise for no apparent reason, like loneliness, depression, sadness, confusion, withdrawal, neediness, or discombobulation. We can even feel sick and weak, often vomiting for months. Our bodies begin to swell and take on a new form until the pains of travail and labor force open our cervix and create a pathway for delivery. Notice how our natural bodies teach us about our spiritual beings. When we are broken over our sin because the Spirit of Truth has awakened our spiritual eyes, our hearts become emotionally bloody. Remember in our physical hearts we have forty thousand neurites

called a heart-brain. Likewise, the number for our spiritual testing is forty. Whatever seeds or words that have been planted in our hearts then begin to flow from our heart on our breath and through a passage way called the cervical or neck. The cervical and the cervices are replicas of each other. One reveals the heavens above and one the earth below. It is when we are broken spiritually/emotionally and whole in our identity in Christ Jesus, at the same time, we can give birth to the living Word of God out of our mouths. The floodgate of truth opens up as our hearts break, allowing our shame and guilt to flow out as the Truth sets us free from the lies that we have held as truth in the strong delusion spoken of in 2 Thessalonians 2:11. In our cries we groan with words that cannot be uttered. We see our judgments, and spontaneous forgiveness floods our souls. God fills us with mercy and love overflowing enough for us and others, beyond measure and beyond our decision-making abilities. This is what I call uncontrollable, spontaneous forgiveness. This is the birthing of the promises of God.

This kind of experience often comes to pass in painful places in our relationships. Because it is spontaneous, we cannot take credit nor boast. Yet we do want to shout it from the rooftops. After living in this way for a while, our senses become exercised like it says in the book of Hebrews. I call this the maturing of the bride. Jesus is coming for a bride who is spotless and without blame. If we are not honorable women in the natural, how can we be an honorable wife to Jesus?

In this kind of reality, the lover of my soul has become my reality and life. I no longer serve Jesus as my master. I am now one with Him as my husband. My heart is filled with passions unspeakable; my thirst for Him is like a deer panting for water. Just as I desire my earthly husband, I cannot resist being with Jesus. These two relationships are alike, yet so different. They both take my breath away and buckle my knees. I am no longer a bond-slave, but rather I am lovesick and cannot resist my lover.

Sorrow endures for the night, where we are blind to our own nature and deceptions. However, it is in our mourning that we wake up and find the joy of our Lord. Note, anyone can rejoice together, but few will suffer together. I have suffered with my spouse and with Jesus. I have discovered that suffering with them no longer feels like I have been robbed of anything. On the contrary, it is an honor to suffer with the ones I love. Jesus said if we suffer with Him, we will reign with Him. I am here to testify that is the truth. In the book of Ecclesiastes, chapter four, we are taught that a wise man abides in the house of mourning. It is only now that I understand this text. When we are broken, we wake up, and He feeds us manna from heaven.

Brokenness can come in any relationship, but earthly marriage is a perfect schoolmaster to teach us how to mature into the bride of Christ. Anyone can learn about marriage and how to get pregnant and how to have a baby. However, until you experience it, it is only head knowledge. When a woman experiences the pain and joys of being a wife, lover, and mother, then she can say she has understanding.

In the mid '80s I found it difficult to consider being the wife of Jesus. It really didn't make sense to me and even sounded creepy. That is because I could not use the natural to see the spiritual. Many years later, I can now discern how the natural, created things in this earth unveil the unseen spiritual things of God. At first, this may seem a little strange. I understand. Remember my son's response when he first found out about sexual intimacy: "Good, you never have to do that again!" As a dad, he doesn't think that is creepy anymore. Likewise, in time, when you experience deep intimacy with Jesus in your heart, you will see firsthand what I am talking about and it will not creep you out at all. On the contrary, you will be overtaken with His love and your life will never be the same.

This kind of love is expressed in the book of Hosea and the Song of Solomon, just for starters. Once you see this in your life, you will notice that these mysteries are in all of creation and all throughout the Word of God.

Of all of the places that God has hidden His mysteries, I am eternally grateful for my husband, Michael, and the gift of marriage. It is through our beautiful union that I discovered my nature and God's nature toward me. The joy of being a receiver, and the overwhelming gratitude that floods my heart at the revelation of being the bride of Jesus, is almost more than I can take. It is beyond my imagination, and my heart overflows. Just the thought that my heart is the place that He formed and fashioned to place his Word in melts me like wax. This understanding has taken my breath away. He has placed Himself in me and He is the life of who I am.

No Longer Dis-Eve'd

I pray that this work has provoked you to go deeper into your heart and discover all that God has for you in the union of physical marriage, but more than that I pray you awaken to who you are as the bride of Christ.

Chapter 11: Uncontained Passions of the Bride

Brokenhearted and weeping on my floor for what felt like hours, I entered into a vision. I was looking across a beautiful field of tall green grass and wildflowers. The bride of Christ was sitting on a large boulder alone. She was brokenhearted and bowed at the waist. Her chest was resting upon her knees as if she was weeping upon her own feet. Her veil covered her face, yet I knew she was weeping, for I could feel her sorrow in my soul. I almost felt guilty for intruding on her privacy. In the distance, I saw a bridge leading to what appeared to be nowhere. As soon as I wondered where the bridge led, I found myself standing on it. The railings were smooth wood, painted high-gloss white. The spindles were ornate and attached to a high arch. Hearing a tinkling sound, I looked over the edge, trying to figure out the reason for its existence. As I tip-toed and bent over the railing, I saw a gentle stream. It trickled and sang as it danced through the grass and wildflowers. It flowed across smooth, rounded stones as it meandered under the bridge, reappearing on the other side. I looked up to see where the water was coming from and realized the tears of the bride had formed it.

A startling roar broke my attention and I turned quickly to see what was making this sound. Again, by wondering, I was transported to the source of my wonder. I was lifted high, and soared like an eagle above a threefold waterfall. It cascaded over a cliff, landing upon the largest boulders I had ever seen. The tears of the bride had accumulated and created this massive waterfall and turbulent river.

In my mind, I asked, *"What is this?"*

I heard inside of me, *"This is the revelation that is coming upon the earth, in response to the tears of the bride. These boulders are the prophets of God who are able to handle such strong revelation. They shall receive it and break it down into many gentle waters. This revelation is too heavy for many. Therefore, there shall be prophets who shall be trained on how and when to release what they are given. The turbulent waters that you see will carry the revelation to the ends of the river where the waters shall be cool and peaceful and everyone feels welcome. This is the promised rest."*

This vision took place in 2001, and it was the first time I had ever seen the bride. Though her face I could not see, I felt her broken heart, longing for her groom and weeping for the entire earth.

Not long after, again while lying on my floor, exhausted in tears of intercession, I saw her. She was standing before Jesus. He was stretching his arms wide to show her all of His kingdom. With fire in His eyes, He spoke of her beauty and offered her up to half His kingdom. Yet, it was His heart that she could not turn away from. There was nothing more important to her than what she saw inside Him.

This vision continued and was quite long, but the point I want to make is that even though Jesus was offering her gifts, she was consumed with His heart alone. This is a true mark of the bride. Inside of Him is her abode, and when you taste of His goodness, you too will understand why she was so smitten by His love.

I have seen her recently on two other occasions. In 2015, she appeared before my eyes, sort of like a mirage photograph suspended in the air. She was dressed in her wedding gown, yet this time without her veil. Floating in the air, a brilliant purple heart pendant adorned her chest, just above the bodice. There was no chain needed, as it remained steady over her heart. The bodice of her gown was also heavily adorned with what appeared to be crushed purple diamonds that glistened in splendor. Her hair was in a beautiful partial up-do, cascading golden curls across her shoulders. The light that shown from her face was so bright, again, that I was not able to look upon her face. I began to cry aloud and told my husband what I was seeing. I was overwhelmed with awe and wonder. We were lying in each other's arms, as I was weeping for revival to fall upon marriages, asking it to sweep across America and to the entire world. Michael just held me and let me weep until I fell asleep.

The next morning, I grabbed my computer and searched for "purple stones" online. At that exact time, a dear friend of mine sent me a Facebook message telling me that God had told her to send me a Scripture in Revelation. When

I looked it up, this is what I read: "Come hither, I will show thee the bride, the wife of the Lamb. And he carried me away in the Spirit to a mountain great and high, and showed me the holy city Jerusalem, coming down out of heaven from God, having the glory of God: her light was like unto a stone most precious, as it were a jasper stone, clear as crystal...the twelfth, amethyst" (Revelation 21:9-11, 20 ASV).

As I read it, I was stunned at the realization that the last foundation was *amethyst*. The purple stones were not diamonds at all. They were amethyst. Filled with excitement, I searched for its meaning. I soon discovered the meaning of this stone was "to be sober minded." "The foundations of the wall of the city were adorned with all manner of precious stones...the twelfth, *amethyst*" (Revelation 21:19-20 ASV). I was blown away. It was testifying to all that I had come to realize in my marriage. It was in the gift of this holy union and through revelation of my judgments that I had awakened from my drunken illusions. I realized that I was drunk with the knowledge of good and evil. I was bound to my addiction of judging myself and others by this standard. I was under the illusion that love was something that I could choose to do and accomplish, as well as expecting others to do the same. I had never faced the truth of my sin nor understood my denial. I was continually running from the pain of truth and hiding in my good works. Because I refused to listen to God through my emotions and wake up to my lifestyle of fear, self-righteousness, and hypocrisy, I was living dis-Eve'd (deceived). "And with all deceivableness of unrighteousness in them that perish; because they received not *the love of the truth*, that they might be saved. And for this cause *God shall send them strong delusion*, that they should believe a lie" (2 Thessalonians 2:10-11 KJV, emphasis mine). I finally understood that living a lie is to be drunk. Now that I had seen the bride, covered in what I now understand as amethyst, I realized that her foundation had become truth, and therefore she was sober-minded; her heart was set on a foundation of amethyst. She was "No Longer Dis-Eve'd!"

The last time I saw the bride was during the feast of Sukkot, October 2016. I knew it was called the Feast of Tabernacles, and I knew a little bit about it, but I had no idea what the water libation ceremony was until I lived it. Before I expound on the vision, let me tell you a little bit about this feast.

The water libation ceremony was practiced during the Second Temple era during the time of Jesus. It was during this ceremony that He declared in a loud voice that He was the living water to be poured out for all to receive the in-filling of the Holy Spirit, who would be to us the river of life. It was in this ceremony that the water and wine would come together as a prayer offering up to God. The people were asking for God to pour out the latter rain blessings upon all flesh. It is a symbol of the water and blood that flowed from Jesus' side when He was pierced. Notice below in the vision that Jesus washed His face in the tears of the bride. This river was a picture of the waters of Siloam. The priest had to draw the waters from the Pool of Siloam. This was a pool near the Mizpah or watch tower near King David's garden. From this tower, stairs went down to the city of David. It was a high place from which the wise one would be sent away and appointed as one to shoot forth and sow seed. Moreover, it also means to send out a wise one like a missile of attack, to spear, and to shoot forth as a branch or a sword. Remember, branch means the bride. This is what Jesus the prophet of the branch (Nazareth) was referring to when He said that He did not come to bring peace but *a sword*. He was speaking of these festival waters and the bride to come. Another meaning is to send one down to loose or liberate.

You will see below that this ceremony was symbolically portrayed in my vision. This vision happened on the exact day during the Feast of Sukkot in the year 2016. I was at a gathering in Chautauqua, New York in the Methodist House. Chautauqua means resurrected body; New York means New Earth; Methodist means river; and House means Tabernacle. This was not the first time that I had discovered that I was living the promise of Ezekiel 36 where God recorded this promise: "And I will put my spirit within you, and cause you to walk in my statutes, and ye shall keep my judgments, and do them" (Ezekiel 36:27 KJV). This word *statutes* is the Hebrew word *choq* and it means appointment, custom, decree, law, measure, ordinance, set time, statute, task, to hack, hammer, engrave, to be a scribe, to enact, to cut in stone, to prescribe, to govern, to grave, to portray, to print, and or to set.

I was again in a vision; I was standing on the shore of a mighty river. Jesus had on riding boots and was washing His face in the river. He was down on one knee, where He could see the water and wash His face, yet having His face turned toward me so that I could see three-quarters of it. I asked Him what He was doing.

With fire in His eyes, He replied, "I am refreshing Myself."

Somehow, inside me I also heard, "I am being comforted."

I was transfixed by the fire and said, "Jesus, I want that fire."

He smiled, and the fire beamed into my eyes and went down to the soles of my feet.

I responded, "Jesus, my feet are burning!"

He reached out and picked me up and sat me on the air hovering above the river. It was then that I noticed I was wearing a wedding gown. He raised my gown carefully, only exposing my feet, and washed them in the river. By now I recognized this river. It was the one in my first vision that was formed by the tears of the bride. As He washed my feet, glass slippers appeared on my feet. He then lifted me up again and stood me on the shore of the river and began to dance with me, twirling me around and around. I began to weep and asked Him to stop. I was too sad to dance. With tender compassion, He continued to twirl me as I told Him of all of the sorrows that plagued the earth. He then stopped, walked me to a large swing under a huge oak tree, set me on it, then sat beside me and held my hand.

Weeping, I asked, "What is taking so long, Jesus? Please come back now. We need You."

Just then the Holy Spirit came over in a flowy blue gown, like one worn by a mother, and Jesus got up and walked away as if they had agreed on something. She sat beside me and took hold of my hand.

I asked, "Where is He going? What is He doing? Doesn't He care?"

Suddenly, I was taken by the Holy Spirit up above the triple waterfall, and I saw Jesus standing under the cascade. As He stepped out from under the falls, the water became His robe. It was sparkling and appeared white as light. Next, I was standing next to Him on the water. He began walking toward the calm, peaceful waters.

He looked at me and asked, "Will you be My Bethesda?"

"Yes," I cried, "but what does that mean?"

"The doorway unto all the nations. A building, a dwelling place."

Then, just as quickly as the vision appeared, it was gone. I felt like I needed to look up the date and write this down. I grabbed my phone and searched. It was the last day of the Hebrew festival Sukkot—the same day that they have the water libation ceremony and "Dance with the Torah."

I was undone. On the same day that Moses had instructed the people, in the same manner I lived in my vision a replica of the water libation ceremony and I danced with the Living Word. After I danced with Him and was taken up on a high place and then down to the waters where He was standing, He asked me to be His Bethesda. I looked up this word in the Bible and became weak when I read the meaning. It means a house of kindness, a pool in Jerusalem. It comes from two words—*bayith* and *chesed. Bayith* means a house, especially a family, a court, a daughter, a door and a temple. He asked me this on the Feast of Temples! *Chesed* means kindness, merciful, to bend low, to implore, to favor, to grant graciously. It took my breath away as I realized that this word was only written in the New Testament one time. I remembered reading it, but while in the vision I had no idea all that was within the word, much less that it had any hidden meaning.

I don't propose to understand all of the meanings of my visions, but I am fully persuaded that Jesus is calling His bride right now. Now is the time and today is the day of salvation. He is asking us if we will dance with Him and be the doorway. He is asking us if we will be His dwelling place. This can only take place in the heart with deep suffering and reigning intimacy. Are you ready? Can you hear Him calling you?

"Come away with Me!"

The bride, knowing and understanding the heart of God, will intercede with a broken heart, uncontrollably. Her heart is compelled to intercede because it has been united with His. Passions burn in her, causing her to cry for His children. We have longed for passion in both our relationship with God and with our spouses. I was sick and tired of loving out of commitment and came to a place where I would rather be committed than to be married out of commitment. Do you long for His heart, not because you are committed to Him but because you are smitten with His love?

Jesus came to give us abundant life, and when I didn't experience that I became angry and could no longer settle—not in my earthly marriage or in my eternal marriage to Jesus. Are you willing to settle? You don't have to. God's promises are true and available to you.

As a wife, a woman longs to live passionately with her lover, becoming the mother of his children. She is willing to fight for passion and intimacy, often being misunderstood and falsely accused. It is not being right that she longs for; it is being intimate.

Intimacy is worth dying for. We are also willing to die for our children. This is the nature of a woman, a bride.

As the bride of Christ, we too are willing to die for intimacy and for the children of God. We are broken over the ones who don't know that God is love and that He loves them. It is not a chore that we do this; it is the very nature of who we are. It is neither a duty nor a sacrifice; it is our honor. Smitten and breathless we follow Him, no longer out of obedience but out of our passions beyond the grave.

Our emotions are the unseen blood that flows like a river bringing revelation, and it cleanses us from all the lies that we received in our hearts as children. It delivers the nutritious milk of compassion and picks up the toxins left behind from the lies of our past. The testimony of our past, experienced in the bitterness and pain in our hearts, expands our understanding of God's suffering love. He cannot resist us in our time of need. So, before time, He came and suffered with us so that when we remembered our sorrows co-mingled with His, He could look us in the eyes and without words convey: "I have never left you, nor forsaken you. I was with you in every sorrow, and I have been waiting for you to come into the garden of your heart. I knew you would find Me, for My Father wrote Me on your heart before time."

It is in this kind of brokenness that we realize our judgments toward ourselves, others, and God. In this truth, we awaken to the reality of our own condition, and likewise we understand others. Judgment has become the fabric that the Holy Spirit used to fashion our garments of humility, thereby delivering us from the pride in our lives.

In marriage, I discovered I am everything that I have ever judged. I have been broken and forgiven and clothed in mercy and humility. My cry has become, "Have mercy on us all, Lord, and give us Your eyes, for my eyes can only see in part. Forgive me for trying to trade You for love and thinking that You would take my bribes. Forgive me for judging You as a God who was dependent on me or indifferent to my needs. Only through brokenness did I see that I was reaping what I had sown, receiving what I had believed about myself, and being what I thought about myself and others. I surrender my name for Your name, my mind for Your mind, my eyes for Your eyes, my emotions for Your emotions, my will for Your will."

I urge you to keep this in remembrance when you are hurting: "The Lord is not slow in keeping his promise, as some understand slowness. Instead he is patient with you, not wanting anyone to perish, but everyone to come to repentance" (2 Peter 3:9 NIV).

God will not remove the tares from your garden until the wheat is mature. He shall wait as long as it takes for you to trust Him with your pain. Remember, you are worth waiting for because He cares for you. He knows you are dark, but He calls you "Lovely."

Postscript

As I typed the last two chapters of this book, I sat sobbing for couples all across the world. I saw myself sitting in a rocking chair, holding planet earth in my arms. It appeared small enough to be my baby, and I held it with such care and tenderness. I was weeping for every broken family, man, woman, and child, who all long to feel loved and desire a loving, peaceful home. I felt the longing for a home where mamas and daddies really love each other, where families laugh over dinner and hold each other in slumber under the covering of the stars each night. A home where God is a part of every word, and His light is the light of their hearts.

I felt my heart whisper softly, "It's OK; you are already loved. I love you. You just don't know it yet; but you are never alone."

God is with us. I am done now. I finished my book. I am sending you my story, and you will soon discover that you are loved, and you will feel it in your hearts.

I could feel my heart exploding with compassion, care, and gratitude for my family, the human race, and our home, planet earth.

May this work open the eyes of your heart and the ears of your understanding. May we all awaken out of our emotional slumber and become sober-minded. May we arise and shine as the beloved bride that Jesus is returning to adorn.

> "For God so loved the world, that he gave his only begotten Son, that whosoever believeth in him should not perish, but have everlasting life" (John 3:16 KJV).

About the Author

Born and raised in Louisiana with her five sisters, Angela cherishes the memories of her life growing up in the melting pot of that area's culture. From her mother, Sarah, came Angela's love of cooking and storytelling; her father, Louis, instilled in her a love of hunting and the outdoors. She can recall experiences with God that took place at the age of four, and she had a supernatural encounter with Jesus when she was fourteen. Over the years, she has forged a unique biblical perspective by digging deep into the significance of words, numbers, creation, and the human body.

In 1985, Angela married her best friend and hunting buddy, Michael Sr. Along with their two adult children, they also presently have four grandchildren.

Michael and Angela are ordained ministers who have traveled together across America, teaching and demonstrating revolutionary truths about the human body and how it relates to our spirituality. Moreover, as an author and spiritual life coach, Angela travels nationally and internationally, bringing her revolutionary work to the world. It is her desire to change the way individuals view emotions, allowing their hearts to heal as they learn to process emotions in a healthy manner.

Angela facilitates over 400 personal sessions per year, with miracles following. Breaking unhealthy life cycles that have been trapped in the subconscious has yielded miraculous healing to numerous recipients. She has seen cancers die, tumors disappear, a dead bladder come to life, PTSD disappear, marriages heal, and symptoms of fibromyalgia and food allergies cease. Her life coaching has set people free from codependent and self-destructive relationship patterns. You can follow her on Facebook, Twitter, PodOmatic, and iTunes.

We are a Christian-based publishing company that was founded in 2009. Our primary focus has been to establish authors.

"5 Fold Media was the launching partner that I needed to bring *The Transformed Life* into reality. This team worked diligently and with integrity to help me bring my words and vision into manifestation through a book that I am proud of and continues to help people and churches around the world. None of this would have been possible without the partnership and education I received from 5 Fold Media."

- Pastor John Carter, Lead Pastor of Abundant Life Christian Center, Syracuse, NY, Author and Fox News Contributor

*The Transformed Life is forewarded by Pastor A.R. Bernard, received endorsements from best-selling authors Phil Cooke, Rick Renner, and Tony Cooke, and has been featured on television shows such as TBN and local networks.

5 Fold Media
5701 E. Circle Dr. #338, Cicero, NY 13039
manuscript@5foldmedia.com

Find us on Facebook, Twitter, and YouTube.

Discover more at www.5FoldMedia.com.